Tributes to Lost Children

Tributes to Lost Children is a report on responses to a survey from 147 families on actions they have taken to honor their children who have passed away. In addition to many wonderful anecdotes that the families shared in their survey responses, one significant observation is that the very act of sharing tribute information can be a tribute in itself.

A few participants commented on the Tributes Survey ...

- *Thank you for doing this survey for all of our children that are gone too soon!*
- *What you are doing here is such a huge step toward helping others know that losing a child is a monumental loss for families, but that keeping our children's memories alive is a wonderful tribute to life and love of family and friends. We want to talk about them. We want to remember them! Thank you!*
- *This is a great idea as I always ask members to share what they've done with the group. I've forwarded this on to some special people who have done some amazing things in memory of their children.*
- *In almost twenty years on this journey, I am always inspired by what other parents and families do to memorialize their children. I think this survey is one of those ways! Such important work you're doing!*
- *This recognition of the importance of our children's lives is so necessary. So many people, if they have not experienced this, do not understand this. Your recognition is a meaningful kindness.*

Tributes to Lost Children

A snapshot of how 147 families have honored their children who have passed away

by Rod Mebane, Emma's Dad

Geneva, Illinois ★ StarshineGalaxy.org

Starshine Galaxy Foundation NFP

Tributes to Lost Children – by Rod Mebane, Emma's Dad

2016 / 134 pp / 26 photographs (grayscale in print)
Starshine Galaxy Foundation NFP / Geneva, Illinois / *starshinegalaxy.org*
ISBN13: 978-0-9908547-0-8 / ISBN10: 0-9908547-0-1 / Library of Congress Control Number: 2015919365

The author extends appreciation to his wife Donna, daughter Sarah, and colleagues Meghan Campbell and Angela Scaperlanda-Buján for their important contributions. Special thanks to Alan Pedersen for his support of this work and for the source of inspiration that he has become.

20 19 18 17 16   7 6 5 4 3 2 1

Dedication

This book is dedicated to the people in families who have lost a child.

The moms and dads of children who have passed away, the brothers and sisters and grandparents, the uncles and aunts and cousins ... This book is dedicated to them. They were not able to complete their work as loving caregivers, mentors, and friends to these children. They were not able to see these children flourish and mature in the ways that they hoped, dreamed, and prayed. All aspects of their losses combine to create a burden of hurt on the heart that never fully eases, an amputation that forever changes the concept of normal.

Tributes to Lost Children *is dedicated to this all too pervasive group – a broad network of souls, including my own, connected in grief over our lost children. I hope that aspects of this report bring some measure of comfort, peace, or renewal.*

Rod Mebane, Emma's Dad

Rod Mebane

Rod Mebane is known for his ability to simplify complex things. In the early 90s, for example, when he was treasurer of Southern Methodist University in Dallas, he decided to study Spanish at a local community college and (for 'fun') ended up publishing *Más Fácil,* a textbook that contains the rules of Spanish grammar in less than 100 pages of text. Rod has made significant contributions applying his sense-making skills in the worlds of nonprofit management, institutional investment, organizational communication, and corporate learning.

Rod came to the subject of 'tributes to lost children' after his daughter Emma – his fourth and youngest child – died in her sleep in July 2011. His survey of the subject stemmed from curiosity about how other families honor their kids who have passed away. When people responded so fully to the survey, it turned into another complex situation that needed to be simplified. That, of course, is the story of this book.

Currently, Rod works as an independent publisher and lives with his wife Donna in Geneva, Illinois, a far-western suburb of Chicago. When pursuing avocational interests, he carves wood, keeps bees, and spends time breathing life into Starshine Galaxy Foundation NFP.

Starshine Galaxy Foundation NFP

Starshine Galaxy Foundation NFP is an Illinois not-for-profit corporation, and application is pending for recognition by the IRS as a §4942(j)(3) private operating foundation. The Foundation's general purpose is: 1) to sustain the memories of deceased children in honorable ways, and 2) to provide assistance to people bereaved by the loss of children who have died. Visit *starshinegalaxy.org* for more information.

Contents

Foreword

by **Alan Pedersen** (Executive Director, *The Compassionate Friends*) i

Tributes to Lost Children

1. **Introduction to the Tributes Report** 1

2. **Meet the Children** 9

3. **Tributes ... To Keep the Children Present** 17

4. **Tributes ... To Remember the Children** 43

5. **Tributes ... To Create Goodness from Loss** 69

6. **Healing Effects of Tribute Activity** 91

Afterwords

7. **Afterwords – A Forum for Sharing** 101

Backstories

A. **Author Notes** 111

B. **Tributes Survey** 115

The 'Tributes Framework' (SUMMARY) 121

Foreword

When my 18-year-old daughter Ashley died in an automobile accident in August of 2001, I needed answers. Of course in those early days I wanted answers as to why it happened, why it happened to me, and how would I possibly survive? I desperately sought out and chased down any resource I could find. I read books, participated in grief programs, and joined The Compassionate Friends seeking answers and support. All of these things proved helpful to me.

Alan Pedersen
Executive Director
The Compassionate Friends

As I grew in my grief and in my understanding of the process of loss and how it affects us mentally, spiritually, emotionally, and physically, I began paying particular attention to those who were finding a quality of life again after the death of their child. Because of my curious nature as a writer and my need to find answers as to how to survive, I asked many questions of those who had found peace and even joy in their lives once again. The information gleaned from these individuals helped shape my early journey through grief and became the basis of what would later become my message of hope.

By emulating what I had learned from others and applying good grief information, it provided an opportunity to share Ashley, our story, and a positive message of hope through music, writing, and presentations to nearly 1,000 audiences across the United States and Canada. I had often wished that I would have more carefully chronicled every morsel of good information passed along to me over the years.

Unfortunately, my gift isn't sorting through hundreds of stories and random insights in an attempt to quantify and simplify the data into an informative and inspirational format. Fortunately, there is Rod Mebane who possesses a giant heart and a brilliant analytical mind capable of creating such a work. In *Tributes to Lost Children*, Emma's dad meticulously breaks down the stories shared with him of 147 families who have experienced the death of a child.

Rod has taken the collective journey of these 147 families and presented his findings to each of us grieving the death of our own child. In my nearly fifteen years walking this walk as a bereaved father, I have not come across such a powerful resource of first-hand information. This book has a wealth of examples of how others not only survived their loss, but also what they did that helped them find their way back to fully living again.

Tributes to Lost Children honors the life of Emma and all the children whose lives inspire so much good work in their memory. This book can benefit all those who are grieving as well as those who care for and work with the bereaved.

Alan Pedersen
Executive Director
The Compassionate Friends/USA

Chapter 1

Introduction to
the Tributes Report

It could not be true.
How could he be here for 24 years and
then irreversibly cease to exist?

— Mary Tyler Moore, Richie's Mom

1. Introduction to the Tributes Report

I have been a dad for a long time. It's my favorite role in life, and I wouldn't trade very many of my dad days in – good, bad, or ugly – because they have all added up to a pretty rewarding life experience. However, without question or hesitation, there is one day that I would turn back in if I could. That's Friday, July 8, 2011. When Emma, my 19-year-old daughter and youngest child, failed to wake up on that morning, I wasn't just a dad anymore. I also suddenly became a *bereaved* dad, and that now is a role in which I will serve for the rest of my life.

Since that fateful day, which turned my world upside-down and inside-out, I began to create what someone called 'altars of remembrance' in Emma's honor. While we have organized a few major tributes to Emma since her death, I have also done a variety of little things to honor her. I published one of her little childhood 'books,' for example. I designed a glow-in-the-dark frisbee as a giveaway for a memorial FUN-Run that we planned. I had one of Emma's art pieces framed for a display in the conference room at my work. Things like that.

A little over a year ago, as I was puttering along in this fashion, I found myself wondering about how other families honor their lost children. I looked into this and, when googling didn't provide many insightful answers, I decided that I would ask some families directly. So, I dusted off an email list that I used in December 2013 to send out a poem that I called *Santa Lost a Child* (which I wrote as a tribute to Emma – one of my 'altars'), and I used that as the initial contact group for what I began to call the *Tributes Survey.*

I didn't know of course what the response would be like, but it turned out that I did not have to add to that email list at all. By the end of a week, 147 surveys had been completed, and that seemed like plenty to start processing. So, I began immediately to sift through the terrific (but somewhat overwhelming) amount of information that people had shared. Now, some 18 months later, this report is the final result of that effort. Pulling it all together was a lot harder than I thought it was going to be.

A	B	C	D	E	F
Resp ID	Child Name	Gender	Death Yr	Age	Cause of Death
1001	Craig	Male	2014	20	natural causes
1002	Jacob	Male	2010	23	short-term illnes
1003	Kelly	Female	2004	15	vehicle accident
1004	Chandra	Female	2002	22	vehicle accident
1005	Julian	Male	2010	< 1	overdose
1007	Adam	Male	2005	20	suicide
1008	Faith	Female	1985	< 1	unsuccessful bir
1012	Chris	Male	2006	21	natural causes
1016	Jermaine	Male	2013	13	other accident
1017	Sean	Male	1996	22	vehicle accident
1018	Todd	Male	2007	31	vehicle accident
1020	Bradley	Male	2000	35	medical complic
1021	Nikki	Female	2002	22	long-term condi
1024	Tony	Male	2009	24	long-term condi
1025	Elizabeth	Female	2002	16	vehicle accident
1027	Jeremiah	Male	2006	26	vehicle accident
1030	Adam	Male	2003	24	vehicle accident
1031	Delaney	Female	2004	3	other accident
1032	Josh	Male	1997	23	other accident
1035	Shaun	Male	2007	24	vehicle accident
1036	Michelle	Female	2008	32	undetermined
1037	Max	Male	1995	18	vehicle accident
1038	Alex	Male	2004	10	short-term illnes
1039	Christopher	Male	2009	39	suicide
1040	Marissa	Female	2007	5	medical complic

Understanding the 'Data'

I was true to my statistical training at first – pulling the survey data into Excel, cleaning up format issues, doing some summary recoding, accounting for missing values, and the like. But, after all that set-up type stuff, when I first pulled back to assess – *what does this group have to say?* – I realized that, for several reasons, my research methods training hadn't fully prepared me for this set of data.

For one, the survey sample was nowhere near random – it favored families who have helped coordinate the *Worldwide Candle Lighting* that takes place in December of each year – and that makes it hard to generalize in any 'statistically significant' way.

For two – and way more important – I had one of those *DUH* moments when I realized that the information that people provided in the survey was not about numbers. It was about stories – 147 sets of stories to be exact, about children who have been lost to pre-mature death ... stories of undying love from these children's families and friends, of things they've done to pay tribute to their kids' accomplishments, memories, dreams, and inspirations.

Then, for three, I was also challenged because some of this is pretty emotional stuff, and at times working through the blend of heart-warming and heart-wrenching detail in the stories was difficult. To give you a taste of what you'll read inside these pages, here's just one example – it's about Kelly, a Marine killed at the age of 22 when the Osprey aircraft that he was aboard crashed during a training exercise. This is some of what Kelly's mom had to share about tributes in his name:

We have Kelly's rocking chair with his last pillow in a plastic bag and his stuffed animal 'Cuddles' (for whom he sent adoption papers off). He loved Cuddles, and I did everything I could for him as a child to make him happy ... I also have Baby Benji in a cabinet for show. Kelly never went anywhere without Baby Benji, and he still wears the shirt Kelly put on him as a child. I have tributes on all walls given to me by special friends, the military, and family. There are so many more tributes – for example, a monument at the Marine Museum done by a group of mothers and wives of men who were in the crash of Ospreys. We had a Foundation in New York. Also, his high school in Cheraw re-named a prestigious award – 'The Spirit of the Brave Award' – to include Kelly's name.

So, now familiar with what I was dealing with, the main task for me became – *how do I put all of this amazing, but pretty 'squishy,' emotional, story-stuff together in a way that makes sense?* And, at first, it was formidable to me. While I could see that each of the vignettes buried in this pool of data was a shiny golden nugget, the whole thing felt a lot like an expansive vat of jello.

But ... persevering ... as I read the stories, and re-read them, I began to see themes. Then, after more familiarity, I saw themes within themes. And the process went on like that for a while, and eventually a sense of order appeared within this database of stories. That order is what now supports the design of the book.

The 'Big Story' – A Patchwork of Love Stories

In the end, this book is the 'big story' – the story of all the stories that emanate from tributes to these 147 children. The consolidated story is a beautiful patchwork of activities stitched together by members of the bereaved community in a way that shows the deep, abiding love that bereaved families have for their lost children.

In the end, this 'big story' is elegant. It is told simply, but there is a lot of content power in each of the simple premises. It goes like this ...

In honoring their lost children, bereaved families are driven by three general motivations:

1. ***Bereaved families want to keep their children present in their lives.***
2. ***Bereaved families want their children to be remembered.***
3. ***Bereaved families want some good to come from their losses.***

Acting on these motivations, 147 bereaved families have undertaken dozens and dozens of amazingly generous, remarkably touching activities that themselves fall into natural groupings that tell an even deeper tale.

I have used the three driving motivations (above) as the three main *Tributes* sections of this book (Chapters 3-5). Then, as you will see early on, the three main organizing principles give way to other layers of organization, and sprinkled all along the way of course are stories from the families (the *Survey Responders*) – the personal accounts that make these children come to life so vividly in our imaginings and in our hearts. (I call this structure for organizing the book the **Tributes Framework**.)

Following the tributes, you can take a quick look at the impact of tributes on the families from a healing perspective – in **Healing Effects of Tribute Activity** (Chapter 6). Here you will see numerous examples of benefits that people have experienced – from acting on an important sense of purpose ... to just hearing the child's name ... to seeing that the child's friends still remember.

Lastly, there is a concluding chapter called **Afterwords** (Chapter 7), which brings some special focus to the importance of telling stories about our children who have passed away.

But, first, let's meet the children.

Chapter 2

Meet the Children

Beyond the door, there's peace I'm sure.
And I know there'll be no more tears in heaven.

— Eric Clapton, Conner's Dad

2. Meet the Children

As I mentioned in the **Introduction**, when I started working with the *Tributes Data,* I quickly came to the view that I was not dealing with a statistical sample of 147 respondents. Rather, I was working with a big bundle of stories – stories about 147 children who have passed away. Parents and other family members openly shared information on things they have done to pay tribute to these 147 kids – to their accomplishments, their memories, their dreams, and their inspirations.

As I've pulled it together, the stories about these children unfold in organized snippets over the pages of this book and, by the end of the book, you will develop a good impressionistic sense of these special individuals – who they are and ways that their families have chosen to honor and remember them. But, here at the outset of the report, it is natural to wonder: *Who are the children? Where did they live? How did they die? How old were they when they died?*

If you read more about the *Tributes Survey* in **Backstory B** (page 115), you will see that I intentionally did not probe very much for personal information, out of respect for the families' privacy. However, I did ask a few context-setting questions that help provide a sense of who these children are in space and time.

The Children

The 147 families in the survey provided first names of 141 children who have passed away. After accounting for duplicate names – such as the five boys who share the name 'Adam' and the two girls who share the name 'Michelle' and so forth – there are 109 unique first names altogether. These first names are featured artistically on the back cover of this book, and they are presented here as well:

Shaun Marissa Curtis Marcella Barry Tiffany Isaiah Jeremiah Shaw Christy Kali Aylah Delaney
Lydia Adam Tony Aidyn Brayton Catherine Shawn Brittany Jimmy Nikolaus Kevin Brooke
Erika Justin Amy Ricky Michael Julian Faith Chris Jenna Lindsay Toni Carmen Craig Hayley Jacob Tori
Christopher Darla Kelly Darcy Kristi Ryan Amanda Michelle Perry Scott Wesley Sheldon
Deanne Jeana Jake Tyler Nikki Emma Alexis Dylan Patrick Joseph
Stephen Matthew Pam Patricia Mariah Robert Kelsey Kira Sarah Logan Ava
Max Jen Jo Carissa Sean Leslie Matt Bradley Gavin Ashley
Raymond Johnathan Anthony Sam Owen Brandon Ellen Todd Brian Aaron Seth Mary Chandra
Nicole Branson Alex David Elizabeth Jett Geoffrey Chad Jermaine Josh Renee Andrew

As you might guess after scanning the children's names, there are many more boys reported on in the survey than girls – the actual split is 62% versus 38%. While I can't reliably generalize from our data set, this ratio is similar to what you would find in the U.S. as a whole. According to National Vital Statistics data, of those children (under the age of 25) who died in the U.S. in 2010, 64% of them were male. The male-to-female imbalance is especially evident during the late teenage years and early twenties.

Addressing how old the children were, the average age at time of death within our group is 18.8 years, however the ages in the survey population ranged from infants (under the age of 1) through to children over the age of 25. The oldest child in the survey was 51 at the time of death (attesting to the perspective that the death of a child can be at any age).

The actual age distribution for the full *Tributes Survey* group is shown in the table to the right.

In terms of where the children came from, virtually all (99%) of the population in the survey is U.S.-based, in 35 different states. The largest numbers of children came from California, Indiana, Illinois, Ohio, and Pennsylvania. To give you a feel for overall geographic spread, all the state names mentioned appear in the 'wordle' shown here, with size of name adjusted by frequency of mention.

Age at Death (n=145)	
Average 18.8 years	
< 1 year	14 (10%)
2-5 years	5 (3%)
6-10 years	6 (4%)
11-15 years	16 (11%)
16-20 years	46 (32%)
21-25 years	28 (19%)
> 25	30 (21%)
MISSING VALUE	2 (MV)

Cause of Death (n=142)	
Vehicle accident	51 (36%)
Other accident	21 (15%)
Homicide	6 (4%)
Suicide	7 (5%)
Overdose	7 (5%)
Military conflict	1 (1%)
Short-term illness	10 (7%)
Long-term illness	15 (10%)
Unsuccessful birth	6 (4%)
Medical complications	6 (4%)
Natural causes	5 (4%)
Undetermined	7 (5%)
MISSING VALUE	5 (MV)

Lastly, in terms of how the children died, the causes are many and varied, and you can see how they sorted out in the table shown to the left. Accidents, as a general category, claimed just over half of the children (51%), and the vast majority of these accidents were vehicular. Illnesses (short- and long-term) made up the second largest (17%) of the overall cause-of-death categories.

The Children's Families

The survey did not generate very much demographic information about the families of the children who have passed away – that was not the focus. But we do know that most of the *Survey Responders* (94%) are in a parent role to one of the 147 children who passed away. (There were a couple of siblings who participated and a couple of grandparents, one aunt, and that's basically it.)

We also know that the *Survey Responders* as a group have been bereaved for quite some time. If you look at the recency of death – how many years ago the child died – the average for the survey population is 10.1 years. Again, as with the children's age at death, there is considerable variability in recency of death – see the table to the right – but the survey group as a whole

Recency of Death (n=145) Average 10.1 years ago	
0-2 years ago	13 (9%)
3-5 years ago	29 (20%)
6-10 years ago	54 (37%)
11-15 years ago	26 (18%)
16-20 years ago	11 (8%)
20+ years ago	12 (8%)
MISSING VALUE	2 (MV)

tends to have been part of the bereaved community for a decade or more.

While there is not much data about the families of these children, there is one thing we know for certain about them: they have honored their children in countless ways. That is the subject to which we now turn – the tributes to lost children.

Chapter 3

Tributes ...
To Keep the Children Present

Grief changes shape but it never ends.
I miss all the great things that will never be.

— Keanu Reeves, Ava's Dad

3. Tributes … to Keep the Children Present

Bereaved families want to keep their children present in their lives.

When my daughter Emma died, one of the immediate effects on me was that I lost whatever sense I had of value and purpose. Suddenly, in a flash, literally nothing seemed important anymore. Yet, early on in this mist of insignificance, I felt an urgent need to do something – and specifically I felt the need to create a place for things related to Emma – photos, mementos, souvenirs, and the like. I started on the day

after Emma died, and it was nothing elaborate. In our family room, the fireplace has built-in bookcases on either side, and I mostly just cleared one of them to create *Emma's Corner*.

This spot quickly established itself as an integral part of our home environment. Someone later referred to my creation of *Emma's Corner* as building an 'altar of remembrance.' It struck me as an odd phrase at first – the word 'altar' seemed a bit too formal – but I grew to like it because to me it suggests an important place of honor, which is how I regard the memories of Emma that I hold in my heart. I am borrowing that phrase for use here, to caption one of the things that many bereaved families do.

Families build 'altars of remembrance' to keep their children close.

Based on my own experience and intuition, I assumed that creating 'altars' of some form or another would be common among families who have lost children, and I asked the question largely out of interest and for confirmation. I phrased it simply as: ***Did you create a special place for photos and other remembrances of the child?***

Not surprisingly, my assumption was correct. Of the 143 responses to this question, 4 out of 5 families (81%) indicated that they did indeed create such a place. Almost half of those who created a remembering place also provided the name that they used to refer to it, and the names were usually direct and succinct, like *Joe's stuff ... Kyle's bedroom ... Mariah's place ... The Geoff Wall ... Beth Ann's angel cabinet ...* and other names along similar lines. I was personally intrigued by a number of one-of-a-kind names, including:

- ◆ ***Beyond the dash*** *– the name given a scrapbook keeping all dedications made honoring Adam since he died in a car accident in 2008*
- ◆ ***Justin changed my life forever!*** *– a Facebook site dedicated to Justin's memory, with over 200 members of family and friends who share pix, stories, and memories*
- ◆ ***Where he parked his truck*** *– a designated spot in the drive where Jeremiah's family erected a NASCAR flag pole and added a memory bench and three fire bushes to honor his memory (and his allegiance to NASCAR)*

Some *Survey Respond-ers* provided general glimpses of special locations where the mementos are ... *in our house and back yard ... inside and outside my home ... pictures around the house ... a private place in my cupboard ... a scrapbook that keeps all mementos of dedications made honoring my son since his passing ... pictures on the mantel ... a bookcase that is dedicated to David and his life ... a wall in my craft room with photos of Jake.*

 **HIGHLIGHT** *A picture is ~~worth a thousand words~~ priceless ...*

> *We were all together in Ireland on St. Pat's day, where David had spent a week with his sister, who was studying abroad. We overlapped for 2 nights as a family; they humored me by letting a waitress take our picture together in the restaurant where we had a meal. The next morn, David left and he died before Sarah got to see him again. That ordinary picture became extraordinary in that it was the last moment we were together as a family.*

A number of other people mentioned having multiple locations:

- *We have pictures of him in several areas in my house that trigger warm memories.*
- *We have a special shelf at home and also at her graveside.*
- *I have three separate areas that I display different things of hers. Each area has similar items. One has angels, another is a pottery piece she made and then a special place for her picture with dried flowers from her funeral in a double frame.*
- *We have numerous photographs of Alex throughout the house. We have a painting of Alex as a young child, on the beach, and pointing to heaven. He looks like an angel.*

And there was this summary from Carissa's mom:

- *The cemetery is her bedroom because that's where she lies but doesn't spend all of her time there. The pole is where her auto accident happened. Carissa's wall is where all of her photos are, and her bedroom has remained her bedroom with anything and everything we've been given in honor of her.*

Others addressed the keepsake items and provided content descriptions that were especially vivid:

- *a wooden keepsake treasure box that I designed to keep his precious things in*
- *a photo quilt that I designed for my son*
- *a quilt made from his t-shirts which I have on his bed and another quilt that hangs on his wall from pieces of his other types of shirts*
- *an oil painting of my son when he was a young boy*
- *I have Craig's ashes, photos, and works of art I have created in his honor.*
- *pictures and music and poems on the website, things of his since he was little in my 'shrine'*
- *pieces of jewelry*
- *I have his army patches and medals that he earned surrounding the flag that I was given at the funeral along with all my favorite pictures from over the years.*
- *There's a beautiful collage I created to put about twenty photos into one amazing space. I added a quote that was important to me as well.*
- *a professional rendering of the family using composite photos*
- *objects my son cherished, toys that he loved and music he had made, writings, drawings, priceless items*
- *silicone dog tags, silicone bracelets and mood pencils (these were popular because they were things the kids were into at the time)*

♦ *photos, mementos, pics of Chris's children and siblings and friends, a collage of all the tattoos his friends have had done in his honor ... some little gifts and tchotchkes that are reminders of Chris ... his handmade shaker box that holds his ashes.*

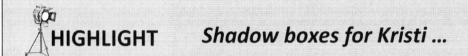

HIGHLIGHT   *Shadow boxes for Kristi ...*

We made shadow boxes of her birth and her death, with pictures, and newspaper clippings, and memories. We put the earrings, necklace, and rings she was wearing in the one with her obituary. The one of her birth has her baptismal bib and shoes and the little cake topper from my baby shower for her.

When I pulled back and looked at the responses of the survey participants as a group, I found that I could imagine a large commingled home, representing many of the different tributes grouped together in one memorial – a **House of Tributes.**

TRIBUTES > KEEP PRESENT > HOUSE OF TRIBUTES

Families dedicate areas in their homes to create special places of honor.

With this image of a **House of Tributes** in mind – a single, consolidated, iconic home – here's a virtual tour of highlights ... a display of some remarkable 'altars of remembrance' in this memorial group home. The tour starts off, of course, in the child's bedroom.

The Child's Bedroom

Our collective house tour begins in the child's bedroom – a space that is hugely important to every kid lucky enough to have one. Here are a few comments that people shared:

- *The special place is Brad's bedroom. His pictures are on the dresser.*
- *It's almost just how she left it ... I can feel her there in her room.*
- *We keep his bedroom as a place to put out things to remember him by. He passed away in his bedroom, so to me it is a good place to have a memorial for him.*
- *I always buy nice things for her bedroom and keep it clean and smelling nice with candles.*
- *In his room above his chest, the wall is filled with pictures and memorabilia along with shelves on the other side of the room holding some of his favorite things.*
- *It took several years, but finally I have her room full of the things that mean a lot to me – photos of her and other memorabilia. This is also a TV room, so I use it often.*

Other Bedrooms

Family members like to use their own rooms, too, as informal 'altars' for some important memory pieces. It's a way to keep certain mementos close – so that they can be seen, sometimes touched ... often at the beginning and end of each day.

- *It's really just on my dresser.*
- *I have a few stuffed animals on my dresser and an area with pictures in my bedroom.*
- *On a cabinet in our bedroom I have put pictures from different ages and some keepsake things that belong to her. It also has some special angel figurines that I have bought or been given.*

Halls & Walls

Now, walking down the hallways in our **House of Tributes**, you may see other memorial displays:

♦ *It is outside our bedrooms in the hallway, so it is the first thing we see before and after bedtime. It holds her special things.*
♦ *It is not a shrine because she would not like that but just an area on the wall with pictures and other remembrances.*
♦ *We have a wall in our dining room with pictures of him and a few of his toys and a poem about him.*

Corners (like Emma's)

You know already from my earlier comments on 'Emma's Corner' that I am a fan of the corner display and, not surprisingly, I am not alone. Other family members mentioned their special corners, for example:

♦ *In a corner glass cabinet … it holds mementos, pictures.*
♦ *I have an Angel corner with angel memorabilia that I collect. Her pictures are there.*
♦ *It is an entire corner with both walls – it is all pictures, poems, some of her special mementos she loved, and things people made for her.*
♦ *I have a corner hutch that has three shelves full of his 'stuff' – pictures, his ashes, stuffed animals, etc.*
♦ *I have a corner shelf with pictures of Branson. I also have printed poems and framed them. I have angels that are on the shelf also, along with an electric candle that has been burning since his death. (The only time it is off is in the case of a power outage.)*
♦ *Our son, David, died in the Boundary Waters area of Minnesota. I asked a friend, an artist, to draw a picture that I could use for the funeral program that would reflect David well. He drew a pencil drawing*

of David standing at a lake's edge, with many significant details – a trillium to represent our 3 children, a pair of loons to represent us (David's parents), 3 pine trees that represent David and his 2 best friends, one of whose father was the artist. That picture hangs in the corner.

Family Rooms

As you might expect, some *Survey Responders* identified the rooms – the family and living rooms – where family members regularly gather, on a day-to-day basis, as 'altar' places for mementos of lost children. Here's a sampling:

- ◆ *It's just in my living room – I have all of his pictures there – on a table in my living room ... Just a living room table with special pictures of him.*
- ◆ *A wall in my living room ... a shelf with photos ... so many pictures ... They cover a whole shelf of a built-in bookcase.*
- ◆ *A bookcase in the corner of my living room. It's the same direction as the TV, so everyone sees it automatically.*
- ◆ *All of the photo boards, posters, poems, and things that people made for Kelsey's service now are prominently displayed in our living room.*
- ◆ *I hung photos on a wall in the living room. It's sort of a*

'gallery wall' – about 50-70 photos, frame-to-frame.

- His table is within our living room and holds pictures, angels, donate life medal, eye bank medal & sometimes special trinkets given to us.
- We have an entertainment center where we have Max's pictures, memory items from him, and also special treasures that we have picked up that have his name on them or remind us of him. We also have his ashes in this center, and he is with us in his/our home – right in our living room.
- We have photos and some of her special things displayed on our mantel.
- In our living room, we have one wall with a picture of Kelly, another one with Kelly and the two other girls that died with her, a picture with an angel on it, and a saying 'angels walk amongst us.' On the mantle, there are many angels.

 **HIGHLIGHT**   *Lighting a candle for David ...*

Sitting on a hutch in the dining room is a candle holder that was painted by another friend. It represents the boundary waters through 4 seasons ... That is our David candle and it is always lit during our family meals together. Why the dining room you may wonder? We always ate in the dining room for our evening meals as I found everyone sat a bit longer, as opposed to eating in the kitchen. When the girls come home, we still eat in the dining room and it feels likes David is with us there – his candle reminds us that his light still shines. Though my description sounds big, it isn't. It is quite understated, and I have been careful to include pictures of my daughters, too. David remains part of the family.

Keepsake Organizers

Independent of room in the house, some *Survey Responders* described special 'organizers' that are used to house important bits of memory, such as:

◆ *A scrapbook that keeps all mementos of dedications made honoring my son since his passing.*
◆ *An oak box with all of the mementos and funeral cards, etc. The family all helped stain and finish it.*
◆ *I have a treasure box that holds all of my keepsakes.*
◆ *I used three-ring binders, and so far I have made five books of priceless memories and reference articles that I can share with others behind me on this painful road. My husband died three years after Alex, and the makings of the books and covers were my life savers.*

Digital Formats & Online Sites

It is also appropriate to include online (or other digital) environments that exist today near the category of keepsake organizers because they provide attractive platforms for organizing various items of importance, especially photos and other media elements (songs, videos, etc.). While there is a small section elsewhere in this report on the importance of Facebook in the grief world of today (30), there are a number of *Survey Responders* who specifically cite online resources as the location of their 'special places' – here are a few references:

◆ *It's a memorial website ... pictures and music and poems on the website*
◆ *Other special places for photo collections are Instagram and Facebook.*
◆ *On the Facebook site, her friends and family leave her messages, and it is great to see that she hasn't been forgotten.*

◆ *At the time of Patti's death, she left three children. In an effort to help them, as well as myself, I created a DVD of her life.*

Given the prevalence of the internet in our lives, many families have naturally gravitated to the web for some of their memory-sharing activities. To the survey question about 'special places' for photos and mementos, about a third of the responders mentioned some web location. While some were not very specific about the sites they used, they indicated a range of functions:

◆ *I didn't create it, but his obituary and guest book have remained online at my request since his death.*
◆ *It contains photographs, famous quotes she liked, Michelle's poetry, her other writings, and links to her favorite Monty Python moments!*
◆ *It's beautiful and heartbreaking – his whole entire life, his short little life, all written down on a few internet pages … I hardly ever visit it, it is so difficult to see.*

When people did mention specific websites, the names included: *freewebs.com, fundly.com, gonetoosoon.org, legacy.com, memory-of.com, virtual-memorials.com, 4everremembered.net,* and *a memorial page on the Allstate Insurance website.*

Survey Responders also mentioned some dedicated, custom sites such as:

◆ *an informational site for my son's memorial scholarship fund*
◆ *a web site that tells about a nursing scholarship we give to those who qualify*
◆ *a worldwide foundation that honors God and memorializes Alex … It is currently still a work in progress.*
◆ *Very sad to create, but it is an awesome tribute that still gets visited over seven years later … We also paid tribute to her on the MADD website, as Brittany was killed by a drunk driver.*

And then, of course, there is … Facebook.

SPOTLIGHT

The 'faces' of Facebook
in the grieving process ...

Nowadays, almost regardless of arena in life, Facebook is likely to be playing a significant role, and that is very much the case when it comes to mourning the loss of children who have passed away.

Facebook in my life? I had nothing against it, but it just was not something that needed to be prominent for me – I felt I had plenty of other ways to stay connected. Prior to Emma's death, I had a Facebook page and a very modest presence, but that's about it. After Emma died, however, I became a huge Facebook fan, virtually overnight.

Fortunately, most teenagers have spent very little time thinking about mortality and, therefore, when one in their age group dies, the friends don't have very well developed tools for managing through the loss. What I saw when Emma died, however, was that Facebook provided a WONDERFUL forum for her circle of friends to grieve openly, lovingly, and with a sense of immediacy and community that was nothing short of profound.

My wife, Donna, has written about Facebook in the context of our daughter Emma's death, specifically addressing the difficult days early on that included visitations, the funeral, house visits, and the like:

Throughout all of this, the great connector was Facebook. Emma's death generated literally hundreds of entries expressing a depth of despair not often experienced by people so young. But right from the start, these kids also tried to get at the essential joy of Emma and her absolute love of life. There were pictures and comments and 'likes' and poems and songs and tags and links. For days, her friends replaced their profile pictures with ones of her or with favorite pictures of them together with her. Eventually, her family joined in and then their friends and colleagues. Emma's Wall became an important part of the grieving process ... **(Tomorrow Comes**, *Donna Mebane, 2014)*

Given this backdrop, it is not surprising that, among *Survey Responders,* there were references to Facebook that demonstrate numerous ways that the platform is being leveraged in the grief context.

A place for remembering:

- *I post pictures on Facebook on special days.*
- *We have a Facebook page we set up with photos of him while growing up.*
- *Every year on Facebook (and via email with those non-Facebookers), I encourage people to hug their children and, because my son was a hugely mischievous little dude, I share what fun mischievous thing we are doing in his memory, and everyone shares what they do in his memory.*

A place for sharing information:

- *I asked my brother to set up a memorial page on Facebook before one of the kids from school did. I now use the page to share many things, including my tributes to Jermaine. (There are currently over 2,700 'likes' on the page.)*
- *My youngest daughter created a Facebook page that anyone can visit to view pictures, listen to special songs, and leave a comment of their own. It provides a way to share thoughts at any time.*
- *We are having a Star Wars R2-D2 droid built in her memory, and people can watch the progress on her*

Facebook page.

A place for staying in touch with the child's friends (and others):

- *We have a couple of pages on Facebook where family and friends can share photos, memories or feelings about Toni.*
- *It is so nice to read the comments from friends, family, and his classmates.*
- *It is really nice to read the messages her friends write and memories they share.*
- *I read and thank everyone who posts a Facebook comment. It warms my heart to read them.*

A place for raising funds for charitable purposes:

- *I created a Facebook page that showcases my creations of art that I believe have been born through Craig sending me guidance. I sell these pieces of art to go into a memorial fund that uses some of the proceeds to help addicts trying to start over again.*

A place for expressing thoughts and feelings:

- *It is our way of talking to Kelly, getting our feelings out and sharing his memory with others.*
- *I write about and acknowledge David on Facebook every time I feel the need. I do this so others who lose a child will know they're not alone and it is ok to share. I also want my loved ones and friends to know it is ok to talk about David – I want him to always be remembered and loved and to make a difference in others' lives. I believe, by being vocal about him, he continues to live.*

Families create outdoor areas around the home for peaceful reflection.

Once you step out of the **House of Tributes** into outside areas around the home, you will begin to encounter lush, colorful spaces and spots designed to hold memories in a rich, bright, living and breathing way.

So, you see that families extend their connectedness with their lost children out the door and into spaces around the house:

- *It is a flower bed at our home. We plant flowers in her favorite colors, purple and blue.*
- *I plant red tulips in my daughter's memory.*
- *I have planted a hydrangea in our rose garden that has always been a special family favorite as she will always be to the family also.*
- *I plant sunflowers every year for him.*
- *We place angels and special flowers in a small area close to our front door. There is also a bench and water fountain there in memory of our child.*
- *We have an area in front of house that has a memory flag with picture, stones with sayings, and various solar lights.*
- *I have a memorial flag in my flower bed. It's a peaceful spot to sit and remember.*
- *Years ago, we planted a small pine tree that Shawn brought home from kindergarten. Since then, we have added many memorial items and flowers to that area.*
- *We began a memory garden in our back yard. It's a work in progress.*

Picking up on this last item, if sheer richness of words shared in the survey is any indication, outdoor gardens represent <u>very</u> meaningful tributes. And, of all the Tributes identified, gardens seem to provide a genuine source of comfort to some people. It's not hard to imagine what the families themselves experience in these gardens:

- *We created a memorial garden at our home, with pond full of koi, a waterfall, and butterfly-attracting plants around the pond.*
- *At the time of his death, we received so many outdoor plants and statues of angels that we decided to start a garden. The day of his accident, Kelly's step-dad, for some reason, cleaned that spot off!*
- *We built a pond with a small waterfall. There's a bench facing the pond to sit and talk with my son … or to journal.*
- *We have made an area in the far corner of our yard. He served four Army tours, so we have a 4-foot banner given to us from American Heroes. It hangs beside 2 pear trees, his favorite fruit. At the foot of his banner is one of his foot lockers with some of his childhood memorabilia, like boy scout stuff, and a bag where family/friends can write notes knowing no one else will read them. My other children built a bench for the area, and we have a*

place for a fire. Being we were not allowed to make any decisions regarding his marker, this is the place I go. There's also a horseshoe pit and a large hammock in the shade. Seven years later, we still have friends and family show up to spend time with Shaun.

HIGHLIGHT

An ever-expanding garden for Alexis ...

After Alexis died, we built a deck on the side of our home. Each year for her birthday, we add something around the deck. In the 12 years since she's been gone, we've added a magnolia tree, numerous angel statues and angel fountains, several flower gardens, a rock garden, a fairy garden, and most recently we've added a swing set and a mud pie kitchen for Alexis' six little nieces. (Even though they were all born after Alexis was gone, they know all about her.)

♦ I have a special memory garden with angels, wind chimes, seashells, walking stones, and a bird feeder. Eventually, it will have a waterfall. It is special because it is for her. I go and sit and talk to her and just think about her and all the good times.

♦ We have a special garden that we have created at our home that we call 'Alex's Garden.' We have planted a border of hydrangeas and a border of green and yellow shrubs. We have planted a large border of yellow lilies, and we have planted a flowering tree. We have a fountain and a plaque there, and we are looking for just the right bench. The garden is situated under and by some tall crepe myrtle trees that Alex loved to climb when he was young. Alex loved the beauty of the outdoors, and we feel very close to him in this place.

- *There is a beautiful rock garden that surrounds our backyard patio. This garden includes a small pond and a waterfall. Shortly after Michelle died, about 30 friends got together, and each brought beautiful large rocks of many compositions. I created outdoor picture frames in concrete that held pictures of Michelle and also her sister Becca. Someone also gave us a Waterfall Japanese maple that we planted at the edge of the garden. The day this garden was created, all of these friends participated, and we laughed and cried together. We always entertain visitors out on the back porch or on the patio. I hand-dug two additional ponds and I landscaped with Japanese maples, shrubs, and ferns. We also regularly plant and place potted annuals in different parts of the garden.*
- *I established a 'Brooke Memorial Garden' in our back yard where I beautify and nurture the garden every year, giving me a place to spend time working and loving the life that comes from it. This way I have a place to visit, other than a gravesite, to spend time thinking about my son, whom I loved and nurtured.*

One mom has worked gardening into an annual cycle: *On our son's birthday in the fall, I plant bulbs and, when spring comes around, the flowers bloom. They are so pretty, and they remind me of our son, his birthday, and the renewal that spring always brings.*

TRIBUTES > KEEP PRESENT > SIGNS

Families associate presence of their children with iconic signs.

Soon after our daughter Emma died, my wife and I – and other members of the family, too – began to notice that cardinals were appearing in odd places and at strange times and, over time, we came to believe (or at least hope) that this was one of Emma's ways of being present with us. As this developed, cardinals became important to us, and my wife has informally assembled an attractive collection of cardinal-related knick-knacks. For another set of reasons, stars have also become important symbols of our daughter Emma.

I did not think much about this but, when I attended the annual conference of The Compassionate Friends in July 2014, I realized that such symbols were very commonly valued by families of bereaved children. The important iconic symbols include cardinals and stars, and also angels and butterflies and flowers and leaves and hearts and fairies and dragonflies and birds and rainbows and raindrops ... the list of things that seem to connect us to our lost children is a long one.

HIGHLIGHT   *David's 'Signature' Bandanas ... Part I*

At the five-year anniversary of David's death, we had bandanas made up with a logo another artist friend designed and sent them to friends. People have taken them all over the world and sent us pictures of the bandanas from everywhere. Last May 28, my daughters were in New Hampshire together and they climbed a mountain on David's Day and I have this wonderful photo of them standing on the mountain holding up this red bandana. It feels like a picture of my 3 children.

The *Survey Responders* referred in a variety of ways to representative objects that are important to memories of their children:

- *I have an Angel Corner with angel memorabilia that I collect.*
- *Butterflies are a symbol and a sign to us.*
- *I now collect angels and butterflies.*
- *We have lots of various angel and butterfly décor in his memory.*

- *I have a red tulip tattoo in tribute to my daughter.*
- *I wear a heart necklace every day that has a cutout of a missing heart. This is the hole that losing Wesley left in my heart.*

Some icons are very specific to the child. For Kelly, for example, it is all about ducks:

- *We display yellow rubber duckies to honor our Kelly. She would always say she was going to be a Duck Farmer. (She was 7th in her class, so for her to say she wanted to be a Duck Farmer was very funny.) Everyday, if she didn't wear an article of clothing that had a duck on it, she would apply a duck sticker. Now … for 10 years, I have been wearing a bracelet with a duck on it.*

And, for Jenna, it is about maintaining the Star Wars connection:

- *Jenna loved children and was a Star Wars fan. So, we are having a droid built in her honor that will be used to bring smiles to sick children in hospitals, libraries, reading groups, or anywhere children are. (We visit with an array of Jenna's friends also in SW character costumes.) Jenna's droid is named R2-JE. Jenna would love this because she was fun-loving and giving.*

Others spoke of sensing 'presence' – not in relation to an icon, but more in a spiritual way:

- *When something strange happens in the house, we always say Joe is saying hi.*

◆ *I openly speak to my daughter when I am alone with my thoughts because I believe that the spirit moves on to a new level and can hear our thoughts. I also believe that the spirit will accomplish tasks that were not completed prior to the passing. My daughter's goal was to reunite her half-brother with his birth family, and she did just that.*

HIGHLIGHT   *Roses for Dylan and Gavin ...*

For any holiday or special event, we put two red roses in a bud vase to represent our boys' presence in a subtle way (but always hoping it will encourage others to speak of them). This was actually Dylan's brother's idea, to put one rose in remembrance of Dylan on the table. So, we continue it for Gavin as well.

At the end of the day – or, if it's late, the very next day – we take the roses to our boys' grave sites. We also usually sponsor altar flowers in our church for our boys' birthdays and angel days.

TRIBUTES > KEEP PRESENT > INVOLVEMENT

Families continue to involve their children in ongoing activities.

To round out this section on how many bereaved families take action to keep their lost children present in their lives, here are a few more activities that responders mentioned.

- *We talk about her each day.*
- *We all talk about him as much as any other family member.*
- *We include Kali in every birthday.*
- *We include her in family functions – we wear her picture button and we light a candle by her picture.*
- *We always rode in the Harley Memorial Day ride. We now carry his banner and hold it on the side lines in memory of him.*

Continuing the idea of involving our departed children in family functions, Isaiah's mom shared a story about her son's 'honorary groomsman':

Our middle son was married two years ago. Being mother of the groom, I did not want to interfere with any of the planning, but I would have been crushed if Isaiah was not somehow included. Luckily my daughter-in-law was very sensitive to our son's loss. There was a candle that was lit in his memory for the service (which was outside), and he was listed as an honorary groomsman. At the reception there was a bouquet of flowers with his photo beside it and an empty chair at the table of the wedding party. It was done tastefully and with loving memory!

In a powerful summary statement, a Michigan parent wrote about the family's continuing involvement of their son with this comment:

We remember him every day and talk about him all the time. There are pictures all over the house, but we don't have a special place dedicated just for him. He is everywhere. It's funny when you ask for specific things, it's hard to say, because he is still such a part of our lives and our journey forward.

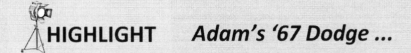
HIGHLIGHT   *Adam's '67 Dodge ...*

My son was in the process of restoring a '67 Dodge when he passed away so my husband finished restoring the car. (You would have to look very closely at the vehicle and then you would see the 'in memory of Adam' we had painted on the car.)

We now take it to car shows and have even won some trophies for it. We do this to keep his memory alive, and it helps to continue to do something we know he would be doing if he were still here with us. His friends will come to the shows to see the car, too, and that make us feel good.

It also is a good way to bring up our child when we meet people at car shows and to get people to know about him and his interests.

Chapter 4

Tributes ...
To Remember the Children

My poor boy. He was too good for this earth ...
It is hard, hard to have him die.

— Abraham Lincoln, Willie's Dad

4. Tributes ... to Remember the Children

Bereaved families want their children to be remembered.

We touched earlier on the desire of bereaved families to keep their lost children present in their lives, and you can see numerous examples of spaces in and around the home that families have designated (and decorated) for private remembering. All of these glowing memory embers help to keep the children close.

There is a companion – and often quite strong – desire on the part of these families to have their children be remembered by others. The important distinction here is that those in the family circle will always remember – their lives have been forever changed – but, with friends and members of the community, the concern is that over time they will forget about the children who have passed away. Families want to preserve the memories and, in their tribute activity, they engage in a variety of activities to sustain them.

As Erika's mom asked, *If I don't keep her memory alive, who will? So, I do, and I love it.* (This particular mom also reported that she has one of the best namesakes of all – *now I have a precious granddaughter to keep her name alive – my little Erika sent from heaven.*)

Another mom suggested that it is really just a way of keeping the children alive in spirit – *Remembering him out loud and sharing about him with others keeps him in my life, if not physically ... I'll take it.* And another sees potential benefit to others – *I hope that by sharing my girl with others, people appreciate their children more.*

And, on the importance of remembering, Stephen's mom offered:

It warms my heart to see Stephen's friends remember him in small ways. One wears his initials on his racing bike. Others wear bracelets I had made with his name and football number. They have asked me to order more because theirs are breaking.

Consider some of the enduring ways that bereaved families sustain the memories of their children who have passed away.

TRIBUTES > REMEMBER > REMEMBERING PLACES

Families designate special places for community remembering.

Much as families have created special remembering places in their yards and near their homes, they have also designated other outdoor spots and spaces for public remembering. These tributes often provide a place where people can go to remember and honor the lost child. They are many and varied and include:

- *a wishing well at the Memorial Park (which helps to support his scholarship fund)*
- *the river in which he was baptized*
- *a bereaved parents garden in Linton, Virginia*
- *Shark Valley in the Everglades – a place where he spent a lot of time with Boy Scouts and family*
- *a mountain park where Ashley loved to go when she was young*

Burial Locations

Naturally, one of the important remembering places to a number of families is the burial location of the children who have passed away.

Some of the *Survey Responders* described things they do to enhance the burial site to make it a special place for remembering:

- *At the cemetery, I framed photos and hung them from metal rose trellises.*
- *We keep up her place at the cemetery.*
- *We plant flowers and decorate his grave site for every season.*
- *Each year that I decorate his memorial stone. I take pictures and share them with his aunts, uncles, and cousins.*
- *Every holiday and on his birthday, I put something special on his grave.*
- *She is in a mausoleum that is on the top of a mountain cemetery. It is a very peaceful and quiet area that is surrounded by a very natural environment. Toni loved to go for walks. So her burial place is a place where we know she would love to be.*

Death Site Markers

Sadly, many of the deaths are associated with specific locations, such as those resulting from vehicular accidents, and some families mark these sites in tribute to their children, with roadside crosses, for example:

♦ *We built a cross at the site of the accident. We leave flowers on holidays and balloons on his birthday.*

♦ *We made a five-foot cross to put on the highway where we lost her. My husband welded the steel together and painted it white. We all decorated this cross and then clear coated it. It still remains just as vibrant as ever.*

In a related situation:

♦ *Some of his friends made a beautiful heart and nailed it to a tree where he was killed.*

And when you think things cannot get any worse:

♦ *We had a cross up near the road for the first five years after Brittany's death. After the third time it was stolen, we took the memorial space away.*

Memorial Benches

When I think of contemplative spots, benches are one of the first things that come to mind, and a number of families mentioned benches in the survey as important to them in providing places to remember. For one, it was *a bench at our local petting zoo that was made in her honor and has a plaque with her name on it.* For another, it was *a park bench on which there is a plaque with his name and dates of birth and death.*

From other families, we learned of *a marble bench at the church ... a seating area with her name on it at a new park in town ... bleachers at the local 4-H grounds ... a bench in a park for people to sit and reflect when they are there ... a bench in her honor on the trail near our house for walkers, runners and bikers.*

One family arranged for two memorial benches in memory of their daughter – one in Steamboat Springs, where the young woman lived at the time of her death, and another near her hometown in Wisconsin. *We found it meaningful for her friends and family to have a beautiful place to go. She was cremated so there is no gravesite.*

And Nicole's mom wrote:

◆ *We placed a granite bench at a park where, in the summer, there is a picnic area, and people walk around it. In the winter, the pond freezes and there is ice skating and kids play hockey. We lived across the street when she was growing up, and she would spend hours there, skating in the winter and playing in the summer and feeding the ducks. At the one-year anniversary, we joined with the family of her friend who also died in the same accident, and the kids' friends got together and planted shrubs around the bench and also a tree in the girls' memory. It is a very nice place to go.*

Memorial Trees & Parks

We saw earlier that trees are sometimes a factor in the cause of death and thus serve as a symbolic marker. On the basis of some other experiences, we can also see that trees provide restorative value to some families.

Examples of trees that have been planted in honor of lost children include:

- ◆ *at her high school*
- ◆ *at parks he enjoyed, at our home, and the cemetery*
- ◆ *at various places including a museum and a school*
- ◆ *a weeping cherry tree in our backyard*
- ◆ *Our daughter's classmates planted two memorial trees with plaques on the campus of their high school. We decorate them around the Christmas holiday.*
- ◆ *My parents planted a tree, and we call it the Nikolaus tree.*
- ◆ *Our subdivision planted a tree in a local park in memory of our son. Each year we decorate the tree with balls and solar lights.*

Patrick's mother shared, *There's a tree planted in the local park with a large rock with a plaque with his name, birth and death dates. It is a very calm place for me to sit and read or just have lunch with my son.*

Families promote the names of their children.

As suggested in this last comment from Patrick's mom and in a number of earlier references, the names of the children – in some sort of printed, painted, etched, engraved, cast, or carved manner – are often associated with their memorials, and they are sometimes memorials in and of themselves. I first encountered this when our city's historical society announced a sale of memorial 'pavers' – 12" x 12" bricks that could be customized – to be included in a new downtown walkway. I was very happy to participate in this fundraiser and arrange for a brick acknowledging my daughter Emma as a 'shining star' for all time.

The satisfaction in this, for me at least, comes from a couple of different directions. The first, and most obvious, is the joy from simply seeing Emma's name (and to know that others are seeing it, too). Seeing your lost child's name in a public place, which is often a beautiful natural setting, evokes a surprising amount of pride and love. The other direction relates to the 'permanent' nature of the tribute – it is a statement, in a way, that provides affirmation that your child existed, that your child was important and should be remembered.

Bricks, Plaques, Notices & Signs

There is no more direct way to promote remembering than by providing a permanent marker with the child's name, and *Survey Responders* provided come wonderful examples of this.

Memorial bricks are perhaps the most common vehicle for preserving the names of lost children ... a brick at the Cosley Zoo ... a brick at Iowa State University ... a memorial brick at Fenway Park in honor of the 100-year anniversary of the Red Sox *(my son's favorite team)* ... a brick paver *at the Italian Catholic Church in the grotto* ... a memorial brick at Angel of Hope Children's, *where Scott's name is seen by many ... a brick with his name inscribed on it at a place they call the 'Friendship Walk' in a local park close to our home.*

Various types of plaques were also mentioned, such as: *a scholarship plaque that hangs in his high school with his picture on it and all the names of the teenagers engraved on it that have received his scholarship every year.*

Noting the importance of seeing the names, a woman who lost her son Alex when he was 10 and her husband Jim three years later shared: *Alex and Jim are all over our town on bricks and plaques to show that they lived and were a part*

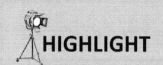 **HIGHLIGHT**   *Michelle stones ...*

I created/invented pocket-sized picture stones which contain pictures of Michelle. I give people we know stones with Michelle's pictures and ask that they leave the Michelle stones at places they think would be places Michelle would love.

She has had stones left by friends at places as varied as a rock garden in Juneau, Alaska, pressed into the bark of a tree in the Canadian Rockies, in a cranny of the wailing wall in Israel, in a cairn on a high hill in the Lakes District of England, and in the Tomb of St. Claire (with the blessings of the Nun who kept the tomb).

I later created stones for other members of The Compassionate Friends (TCF) with pictures of their children. Seeing the face of a bereaved parent when I give them one of my handmade memory stones that contains a picture of their child is priceless!

of our town and other important places. Jett's mom keeps Jett's name alive when she donates: *When stores ask you to donate to a cause, I always write in loving memory of Jett on the papers.*

Published notices were referenced, such as this from Ryan's mom, I *have a memorial in the paper each year which his friends tell me they look forward to seeing.* And Aylah's mom is a proponent of car bumper stickers – *It's so important to get her name out there.*

In a similar vein, Owen's mom wrote, *We have had shirts made that have his name on them and a meaningful verse on the back. Whenever we wear them, people comment on them. We like it because it gives us a chance to talk about him.*

People, Places & Programs

Beyond names (and dates) fixed in wood, metal, stone, and paper, there is a variety of other activity to sustain the names of children who have passed away.

As suggested earlier, one of the most gratifying form of naming is passing the child's name to a new-born in the family, as Carmen's sister did when she *named my son after him,* and as Joseph's mom reported, *my grandson is named after him.*

One family reported naming a star after their lost son. Other naming situations that *Survey Responders* mentioned include:

- **The Justin Payne Simmons Memorial Playground** at the church – *Justin's only job he ever had was working with the children in the nursery at church*
- **Emma's Tribute Swim Team** – *Emma's Hospice nurse is a swimmer and asked if he could name his swim team 'Emma's Tribute' to honor her memory in the Swim Across America cancer fund raiser.*

♦ **Marcella's Closet** – *When I was finally able to pack up her clothes, I donated them to the high school she attended. The ladies in the office pushed the idea of having 'Marcella's Closet' filled with clothes for those in need. The board approved it and 'Marcella's Closet' is in her honor.*

♦ **The Cpl Kelly S. Keith, USMC Memorial Highway** in Cheraw, SC – *I called our Representative and asked that a portion of the highway in his hometown be named after him. Our Representative said he would be honored, and from there it happened. Now friends and family have adopted the highway to pick the trash up every quarter and we won an award for our dedication and hard work towards this special 8-miles memorial highway. I live in Florence, but love going back to Cheraw and riding on 'his' highway. I told them Kelly was 'the king of that road.'*

TRIBUTES > REMEMBER > EXPRESSIVE WORKS

Families create expressive works that are inspired by their children.

A number of different aspects of responses to the *Tributes Survey* touch on the importance of talking about our departed kids, of telling stories about them, of creating works of art as a way of sustaining their memories.

One person simply referenced *graphics, designing memorial photos*, while others were more descriptive of their creative activities relative to children who have passed away. Here are some great examples of expressive art in various modes:

♦ *Painting … I started painting after we lost her, so I painted angel wings and butterflies. I've since grown into many crafts, and there is always some symbol of Carissa, whether it be a butterfly, angel wings, or whatever I feel at that time.*

- **Restoring** … *Right now I am in the progress of repainting all the beautiful Angels that were left at her headstone. They were all bought with love but had faded by the sun. I am giving them facelifts and bringing back their beauty. And I remember Kristi with every stroke of the brush.*
- **Storytelling** … *I talk about him and tell stories to the family who never met him.*
- **Writing** (noted by several different responders) … *We wrote newspaper memorials in the town she passed away … I wrote a letter that I sent out to 50 family members and friends … We put a tribute each year into our local newspaper with a picture of David and a quote that has inspired us that year … I write poems in my son's memory.*
- **Multimedia Presentations** … *We created videos of his life … slideshows with beautiful music and our most favorite pictures of him.*
- **Poetry** … *I write poems and have a gathering for her birthday and her angelversary. In the beginning, I invited a lot if people to the cemetery and played music, read poems, and gave some of my small crafts I've made. I've also ordered puzzles and calendars representing her.*

TRIBUTES > REMEMBER > MEMORIAL ACTIVITIES

Families participate in memorial activities for their children.

Beyond the funerals and memorial services that occur soon after a child passes away, a number of responders mentioned other services and activities that are held to remember the lives of their kids who are no longer with us.

The most frequently mentioned type of memorial service is the powerful and wonderfully connecting *Worldwide Candle Lighting* that occurs each year on the second Sunday in December. It is organized under the auspices of The Compassionate Friends to enable people 'to light a candle for all children who have died.' (See more information on this wonderful candle lighting activity at the end of this chapter, beginning on page 64.)

'Memory Walks' were also mentioned – particularly those held in conjunction with bereavement meetings and conferences (for example, *I participate in annual Walks to Remember*) – and, in general, many other kinds of services are held in memory of children who have passed away.

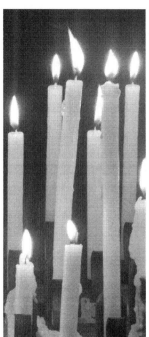

Here are just a few that were mentioned by *Survey Responders:*

- One family, whose child was the victim of violent crime, honors him regularly *in a statewide Victims' Rights program held in April of each year.*
- Another family had a son named Shaun, who served four tours of duty in the Army, and was killed by a truck when he was crossing the street. As a family, they used to participate in the Harley Memorial Day ride. Now, they *carry Shaun's banner and hold it on the sidelines in memory of him.*
- On the first anniversary of Brad's death, his family *held a service at his memorial stone, and his ashes were buried. It was very, very special.*
- *We have an anniversary mass each year. After mass, friends and family gather and bring flowers to the cemetery. We tie ribbons on the tree at his grave. Sometimes we play music, recite poems, or share stories. After the cemetery, we get together for a meal.*

One family organized a one-of-a-kind memorial event to honor Christopher. They called it *Chris's Ride Home* and, according to Chris's mom, it was *a motorcycle rally of local riders who completed Chris's ride from the site of the accident in Saratoga back to Troy. His closest friends and I led the procession in a '74 Ventura that Chris had restored.*

Another family has a private memorial service each year that gets its uniqueness from a coincidence in naming. The family, in California, had twin boys – Wesley and Ashley – and Wesley was killed in an auto accident. It so happens that there is a winery near their home called, *'Wesley Ashley Wines,'* and they *go there every year on their birthday to drink a toast to Wesley.*

HIGHLIGHT

David's 'Signature' Bandanas ... Part II

David wore bandanas a lot. He looked awesome in a tux or a flannel shirt and could pull both looks off brilliantly. But, if he was wearing a flannel shirt, he often had on a bandana. The day before his funeral, the class below him, he graduated in 2006, graduated and because he had many friends in that class, many wore bandanas to their graduation ceremony, tied around their arm, neck or head.

On the 5th year anniversary, we had bandanas created and they are beautiful. One of his friends, a graphic design artist, created a logo that included a trillium, musical notes (David was also a musician), pine trees and a canoe, all creating a circle. In the middle of the logo it says 'may David continue to inspire you to live your life with courage and love.'

I'm collecting all the photos folks take and post on Facebook and making a book of them. David's bandana has been all over the world.

Families commemorate days that are special to their children.

I expressed my opinion in the Dedication to this book that, with bereaved families, there is a sense of 'unfinished business' because their children passed away before they could live a full life. One of the ways this 'unfinished business' is manifest is that bereaved families continue to acknowledge their children's special days in very special ways.

Birthdays are still important. Christmas is still important (for many). And now there is the added 'special' day related to the anniversary of the child's death – what some call the 'angel day.' Let's consider the last of these first.

'Angel Days'

When I was at the hospital on the day of my daughter Emma's death, the assistant coroner commented that *God must have needed a beautiful young angel.* Honestly, it did not bring much solace at the time, but it hit home in making me realize that my daughter is indeed my angel now.

Not long after becoming a member of the bereaved community, I learned about 'angel days.' I also heard the terms 'angelversary' and 'heaven day.' But, regardless of the words that are used to describe it, the day of their child's death is necessarily a pivotal date in that family's history, and families acknowledge the day of death in deliberate ways. While not 'celebrated' in the normal sense, the importance of the child's Angel Day is acknowledged publicly by many.

HIGHLIGHT

Honoring Jenna's love of travel ...

Since Jenna was cremated and had planned to travel the world writing, we have spread her ashes on 6 of the 7 continents around the world:

- *Namibia, Africa over Victoria Falls*
- *Steamboat, Colorado at Fish Creek Falls where she was living at the time*
- *Nachi Falls in Japan where she had visited as a Japanese major in college*
- *Australia's Great Barrier Reef and Sydney Harbor*
- *Iguana Waterfall in Brazil, and*
- *McMurdo Station's Meditation Cross in Antarctica.*

My husband and I will visit Europe together to finish her trip in the Mediterranean Sea. We are making her love of travel continue in water sources around the world.

Some families are intentionally active on Angel Day. From one: *We try to travel as a family on the anniversary of his death.* From another: *Every year on his Angel date, the whole family takes a vacation.* Another family mentioned a specific annual activity: *Every year on his anniversary, we climb Hawk Mountain – a local mountain – and get as close to heaven as we can. As we watch the birds migrate, we pray that they will take our love to our son.*

Other families find a nearby gathering place for reminiscing. For example: *We serve a dinner of his favorite foods on his anniversary and invite old friends over and tell funny stories.*

One mom values some alone time: *I go on long drives WITH him every year on his death-day (and birth-day) so that we are together without anyone telling us what we should do.* And another mom describes how her family organizes Tiffany's Angel Day:

● *At first we stumbled a lot, but Tiffany's Angel date and my granddaughter's birth date are the same day – exactly 6 years and 12 hours apart. It is now an honor to have our granddaughter's birthday party first and, at the end, we do a special cake with all of us telling one thing that Tiffany had done in life (sad, happy, meaningful, etc.) so that the grandchildren learn who their aunt was and are able to honor her. Then we all send our kisses and love to heaven for Tiffany while the granddaughter blows out her candles.*

And here's an account of a graveside gathering:

● *On his death date, immediate family and his closest friends meet at his graveside. I usually read a poem I have written, thank his friends for being there, talk about what he meant to each of us, and we celebrate his short life. I lay red roses – one each for the number of years he has been gone and one white rose to represent the recent year. We each have a balloon that we write messages on and release them along with a Chinese Lantern. I get red heart confetti and Jeremiah's niece, who is ten, gives everyone a handful, and we sprinkle them on and around his headstone and grave ... The love and respect his friends show after eight and a half years is salve to my broken heart.*

Birthdays

In contrast to Angel Days, the events that families plan for birthdays tend to be a little more celebratory in nature. Not surprisingly, many families – thirty or more – specifically mentioned birthdays as one of the key times they use to remember and to offer tributes to their lost children.

In mentioning birthdays as a special time, some families simply mentioned that they celebrate it. Others referenced such celebratory features as *having yard games and cupcakes ... planning a fun activity – water park, bowling, movie, etc. – with our other children in honor of his special day.*

Families mix it up a bit with special activities and themes, as indicated in these snippets:

- *We throw a big birthday party for friends and family.*
- *We share cake with family on her birthday.*
- *We have a birthday dinner with family around Mike's birthday.*
- *We go to his favorite restaurants. His closest friends are invited and it's our treat to them for being such special friends to him and we reminisce about fun times, with lots of laughter.*

- *Birthdays are hardest, behind the anniversary of losing him, so we go to his fave place and I tip extra big, in his honor!*
- *We remember his birthday (and his 'angelversary') on Facebook.*
- *We celebrate her birthday and speak of her accomplishments as a nurse, sister, friend, and daughter.*
- *Her symbol was the ladybug, so for one birthday we ordered ladybugs online and released them at the Angel of Hope.*
- *For Dylan's June birthday, we have a gathering in our backyard and have a 'Dr. Pepper toast' and some of his favorite treats … Since Gavin's birthday month is April, we have the gathering inside because it is still cool outside, but we have similar treats along with a 'Mountain Dew toast' because that was his soda of choice!*
- *She died three months before her birthday. So, we had a birthday celebration of her life that first birthday. We had it at our house, and her friends came.*

And some activities are charity focused:

- *We donate flowers at church for her birthday.*
- *I organised a charity 21st birthday party for my daughter, and all her friends came and made it very special.*
- *We use social media and get the community do an act of kindness on her birthday in her memory.*
- *Every year, for our son's birthday, we do a supply drive for the PICU (pediatric intensive care unit) and collect socks & chapsticks and other toiletries for children and family members.*
- *We had a big birthday party for her 13th! We took donations for a group in our area that has birthday parties for children in homeless shelters or in foster homes.*

But, regardless of designated activities, families consistently recognize birthdays as important opportunities to assemble family and friends in celebrating the lives of the kids who have passed away. I'll close with this one:

🔻 *For Jermaine's birthday (two weeks after he passed), I invited everyone who knew him to the lake where he went in the water. I asked everyone to bring flowers and to line up along the water's edge, and we all threw the flowers in the lake for Jermaine. Later, we lit off 50 sky lanterns. It was gorgeous and beautiful and uplifting.*

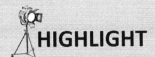 **HIGHLIGHT** *Memories can grow like petunias …*

On the morning of his birthday, I decorate the park bench with a birthday balloon and set out two flats of plants, usually petunias. I also set out a framed photo of him along with a brief biography, also mounted in a frame, and in that biography I invite passersby to help themselves to a couple of plants, take them home and plant them and, as they grow, I ask them to remember Michael. I say how we loved him, how much joy he brought to our lives, and how much we miss him. At the end of the day, I collect everything from the bench and any plants which might remain. Usually there are only a couple … This year I intend to set out perennial plants rather than annuals.

Christmas

For a fair number of the *Survey Responders,* Christmas is included among their children's special days and, not surprisingly, these families adjust their holiday routines and traditions to include the children who join them in spirit. Here's a sampling of some Christmas-related activities that people mentioned in the survey:

- *We put a small tree at his grave at Christmastime.*
- *We get an angel or butterfly ornament for Nikolaus every Christmas.*
- *Each Christmas Eve, our entire family goes to Alexis' grave, and we sing Christmas carols. We also decorate our Christmas tree with angels.*
- *Every Christmas Eve, I host a dinner for my family and Michael's friends. After ten years, they still come. Now several are married with small children. It is the highpoint of my year, and I cherish it. It's as close to having him with us as possible.*

Helping needy children at Christmas is a theme that connected a number of families. For example:

- *For a Christmas benefit, I 'adopted' children with the same name as my daughter's and bought gifts for them.*
- *Every year we adopt a child for Christmas that is the age Geoff would be and provide the presents.*

Candle Lighting Services

Unrelated to Christmas, there is a worldwide event that occurs on the second Sunday of December that is widely supported by members of the bereaved community. It is called *Worldwide Candle Lighting.*

It is organized and sponsored by The Compassionate Friends (TCF). TCF explains on its website: *Worldwide Candle Lighting unites family and friends around the globe in lighting candles for one hour to honor the memories of the sons, daughters, brothers, sisters, and grandchildren who left too soon. As candles are lit at 7:00 p.m. local time, hundreds of thousands of persons commemorate and honor the memory of all children gone too soon.*

Many *Survey Responders* referenced their participation in the *Worldwide Candle Lighting,* and here's a sample of some elaborations that several offered:

- *I just started this past year with our first Compassionate Friend's Worldwide Candle Lighting service allowing all of us who have lost a child to share memories and speak their name.*
- *At the candlelight ceremony at a local church on the second Sunday in December, which we have been doing for 10 years now, we include the siblings and even us parents have had a part in the ceremony. As you like, you light a candle for your loved one and tell about them. We also have a picture of the child on the big screen.*
- *Beth Ann was declared brain dead on December 24th, so at my church we join a candlelight service in memory of all lost children on the second Sunday night in December. I also go to parents locally who lose children and take a rub stone for them to keep in their pocket throughout the day leading up to the funeral and visitation.*
- *I prepare the annual slide show for the Annual Candle Lighting service for the Sandy Springs chapter of The Compassionate Friends. I have been doing this since 2008, and I feel like I know all the children whose photos are included.*

The *Worldwide Candle Lighting* is an incredibly connecting event that many responders look forward to each year.

SPOTLIGHT

Balloons to heaven …

The main snapshot on the cover of this book shows a group of family, friends, and neighbors preparing for a balloon toast to my daughter Emma on the evening after her funeral in July 2011, and I found this to be a very moving way to connect personally with our lost loved one. In describing activities in the *Tributes Survey,* dozens of families also reported a 'balloon launch' or a 'balloon release.' Here are some indications:

Balloons are sent … on different days …

- *on their birthdays*
- *on their angel days*

in different places …

- *at his graveside on his first birthday after his death*
- *at his graveside this past weekend marking the 10th anniversary of his death*
- *at our local Angel of Hope*

and include …

- *love letters on balloons for her angel day and on her birthday*
- *many family and friends wrote messages on the balloons*

- *balloons to heaven with messages written to him so he knows he's not forgotten*
- *with a paper inside that has her photo, birth date, angel date, and a poem she wrote (we did this on her birthday several times throughout the years)*

Here are some other balloon-related anecdotes that the *Survey Responders* shared:

- *A yearly balloon release and gathering on his angel day provides time for his friends to come together.*
- *This was especially helpful to the young children in his world.*
- *We held a special get-together for his loved ones and had a meal, showed a video, had tons of balloons to release.*
- *On her birthday, usually about 15 to 20 of us go to the cemetery and release balloons, have birthday cake, sing, the kids play.*
- *On Michelle's birthday, we always buy some helium balloons and release them in her honor ... Michelle has enjoyed releasing and watching balloons until they disappeared in the sky since she was a small child.*
- *On Easter Sunday, Chris would have turned 27. We held a picnic in the local park, with over 50 friends and family members gathering to write messages of love to Chris on helium balloons and release them together into the sky.*

Chapter 5

Tributes ...
To Create Goodness from Loss

We didn't want our son to have lived in vain.
[ON LAUNCH OF A FOUNDATION TO EDUCATE
CHILDREN ON THE DANGERS OF DRUGS]

— Joanne Woodward & Paul Newman, Scott's Parents

5. Tributes ... To Create Goodness from Loss

Bereaved families want some good to come from the loss of their children.

Families try in various ways to have some good come from their losses, as hard as that is for others even to imagine. Here's an example of a few activates that Alex's mom mentioned: *We are continuing to help others in Alex's memory through our volunteer work and our daily lives ... I am continuing my work with Make-A-Wish, which helps children ... We donate Bibles, and I organize fundraisers at my church for recognized Catholic worldwide relief agencies. We are also establishing a scholarship fund.*

I have organized the various activities that respondents shared along a number of theme-lines that headline the sections that follow.

Families donate to meaningful causes.

Many *Survey Responders* reported that they make charitable contributions to a variety of causes, programs, and activities in honor and in memory of their lost children. The generosity is typified by this comment from a South Carolina mom: *I give money in his name as often as I can. I hope to be able to continue to do that as long as I live.*

Here are some specific charitable actions that loved ones have taken:

- Helping *to pay expenses for a benefit dance at the* **high school**.
- Donating *in honor of him to the* **college** *where he went.*
- Donating *many children's books to the* **local library**. *(He was writing his own books.)*
- Donating to the March of Dimes.
- Donating *(by his older brother) money yearly to our local* **YMCA** *in his memory.*
- Donating *a Records Board at his* **high school**. *He had 2 records at the time of his death. (He was also a 2-event state champion in swimming his senior year.)*
- Sponsoring *a* **day of programming** *on our local radio station in his honor.*
- Giving *books and toys to the* **hospitals and clinics** *where she visited during her illness. We were on the receiving end so much and like to give to others in her memory.*

HIGHLIGHT *Timing is everything ...*

When Nicole died, people gave us some money which we added to what was in her bank account. We kept that money for many years waiting for the right thing to come along, and it did a few years ago. A friend of mine, who lost her son, had a great niece who was a fantastic gymnast in high school but was diagnosed with bone cancer in her leg. Her leg was amputated at the knee. We felt called to give the $3000 we had saved to Brenna to put toward her prosthesis. Brenna had to give up gymnastics, although she tried hard to compete and is now a champion snowboarder. She is an amazing young woman and I know Nicole is cheering her on.

- Making *donations to* **Locks of Love** *and* **Capital Humane Society**. *Chandra had cut her hair and donated it to Locks of Love. Also, she loved animals, and we had gotten our family dog from the Humane Society.*

- Giving *money to a charity in Nicole's name to build a* **house in Haiti** *for a family who had none. We have a beautiful plaque with a picture of the family and their new home. It states it was built in memory of Nicole.*
- Helping *a boy with* **autism** *and* **cancer** *get a new pair of corrective lenses*
- Making donations of *blood two times and planning a blood drive with the* **Red Cross** *in Jermaine's honor this July.*

Some mix it up a bit and spread their support:

- *Every June (his death month), we choose a charity and give money – a multiple of the age in years he would be at that time.*
- *My daughter and I contribute to many charities either through direct donation or through walking/running 5Ks, marathons, etc.*

As suggested earlier, the intended purpose of the gift is often pretty clearly connected to the child in some way – usually related to the **child's interests** or the **child's cause of death**. For example:

- *We have an ongoing tribute at our church. Our son loved his Children's Bible and we donate Children's Bibles every year to the Kindergarten class at the church.*
- Little Emma from Indiana drowned before her first birthday. With a focus on babies, Emma's parents indicated that they *periodically make donations to a local program called Books for Babies, which makes sure every new baby in our county has a new book, with a letter that explains to new parents the importance of reading with children, even newborns!*
- *I have done different things on different years. One year, I gave a donation to a no-kill animal shelter in Washington. He was a huge animal lover.*

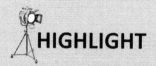

HIGHLIGHT

Maintaining the Chippewa River State Trail ...

We adopted a portion of the Chippewa River State Trail and maintain it by keeping litter picked up. Some years, around the anniversary of David's death and around his birthday, we have organized folks to come and help us clean it up. But the last couple of years we just walk various sections ourselves and keep it tidy. David loved to ride his bike and loved the out-of-doors, so it helps us to get outside and do something that honors him in very ordinary ways. Connecting with nature in this way is always very healing for us and can help bring sunshine into our day, no matter what the weather.

- *We take gifts to the Children's Cancer Center every year on her birthday. She was a pediatric nurse. They are our birthday presents to her.*
- One mom is an artist and sells art online that is inspired by memories of her son, Craig, and she donates *a portion of the proceeds to help addicts trying to start over again.*
- *We have made monetary donations to nonprofits that touched our lives – Ronald McDonald House, Make-A-Wish Foundation, Songs of Love Foundation, To Make A Child Smile Foundation, and others.*

Then, of course, there is the most personal of life-giving donations, as reported by Chris's mother:

- *We donated his corneas to two women.*

Families contribute to charitable activities related to their children.

Over and above any charitable giving, the families reported involvement in a large variety of charitable activities and events. To give you an idea of some specific situations, I have organized a representative list of actions mentioned by the *Survey Responders* in the following two clusters:

Awareness Activities

Some activities are intended to raise awareness about various conditions and causes that might prevent child deaths in the future, such as these reported actions:

- *walked in the AFSP Out of The Darkness Walk every year. It raises awareness for suicide prevention*
- *participated in the Leukemia Light the Night Walk*
- *belonged to a group called PAST (Parents Against Speeding Teens) and we did a walk*
- *spread the word about eye & tissue donation by wearing shirts that say my son was a donor*
- *put together an event in March (Colon Awareness Month) where I tell her story and her doctor gives a presentation on colon cancer and colonoscopy procedure*

Fundraisers & Campaigns

Other activities are more directly focused on encouraging others to action, including raising money for important causes:

- *started a 'be kind' campaign in Ava's honor*
- *raised money for drowning awareness*
- *hold a memorial blood drive every year on Tony's birthday*
- *sponsor a triathlon in Todd's memory ... he had been a triathlete ... he was returning home from a training session at the time of the accident*
- *organize an annual Gala dinner dance*
- *helped in a fundraiser for American Family Children's Hospital*

One mom mentioned two different fundraisers that they sponsored to help out the family of her son, Chris, who passed away in 2013: 1) *a bowl-a-thon – a great fundraiser for the kids attended widely by many friends and families and all the children, and 2) a hard rock benefit show at local hardcore venue that Chris enjoyed – several local bands played to benefit the fund for his kids, and it allowed his friends to gather in remembrance of good times.*

HIGHLIGHT   *Fundraisers for organ donation ...*

Lexis' Angel Sale — *Alexis was an organ donor, and her birthday is in April, which is Organ Donor Awareness Month. So, to celebrate her life, our family hosts **Lexis' Angel Sale** each year on the Saturday after Easter. We sell plants, crafts, garage sale items, and jambalaya dinners. We also host a blood drive on that day. Proceeds from the sale go to **Donate Life Louisiana** to help promote organ donor awareness.*

A rose ... and a racer ... in support of organ donation — *Because our son was an organ donor we yearly dedicate a rose in our son's honor on the Donate Life float in the New Year's Day parade, and we also sponsor NASCAR racer Joey Gase who races in support of organ donation.*

TRIBUTES > DO GOOD > OUTREACH

Families reach out to others to serve important purposes.

In other parts of this section, we have seen indications of remarkable generosity on the part of bereaved families — specifically in terms of their financial contributions and their participation in charitable activities. We also see many who evidence great generosity through gifts of their time and energy, devoted to causes important to the children they have lost.

Let's take a look at some of the causes mentioned to get a feel for some of the underlying factors. Here are some of the topics that family members are addressing with their personal stories of loss and grief:

Drunk Driving

- *I speak at Erika's high school before the prom every year on safety and not getting into a car with impaired drivers.*
- *I speak every month to first time DUI offenders and tell Chad's story.*

Vehicular Accidents

- *I now go to high schools across our state and tell Justin's story. I go with a group called 'VIP for a VIP' – Vehicle Injury Prevention for a Very Important Person.*

Drug Abuse

- *I offered volunteer spiritual services to a local drug rehab program for kids 13 to 18.*

SIDS

- *I speak about my daughter so that others can use her as an example when speaking to their own children or grandchildren. It is exactly what she would want and is the greatest tribute by saving someone else from the same loss.*

Carbon Monoxide

- *We remind people to keep their carbon monoxide detectors up to date and to get rid of them if they are older than 5 years, but more importantly, to have their furnaces and fireplaces properly installed and maintained by a licensed professional.*

TRIBUTES > DO GOOD > GRIEF SUPPORT

Families provide grief support to help others (and themselves).

This is the way Isaiah's parents see it: *Support from other parents going through this experience is the thing that got us through. You do not feel that you are alone in this situation.*

It is clear that one major way bereaved family members give of their time is to help those in the same lifeboat – others who are dealing with the loss of a child. Here are some examples:

- *I facilitate child loss groups at a local hospice.*
- *I created a support group for other bereaved parents and facilitated that for a number of years.*
- *I started a support group for grieving parents. It's called 'Friend to Friend,' established in 2006. We also have a Facebook page and do memorial events.*
- *I created a blog this year to help others know they are not alone in their own grief experiences.*
- *We sponsor the AngelsAcrossTheUSA website and tour bus.*
- *We (our family) have worked at Camp Francis, a camp for grieving children that Darcy was very involved in. Also her sister and I have worked at the teen camp for grieving teens, now called Darcy's Hope.*

As mentioned in the Introduction, there is a high representation in the survey of people who have been involved with The Compassionate Friends (TCF) organization. Therefore, it is not surprising that a number of people mentioned their TCF involvement as part of their own tribute-related activities. As one suggested, they are motivated by *giving back to help others who just found themselves on this journey without their child,* and they find solace by seeing *we are not alone in going through this tragedy.*

These TCF volunteers give back in a variety of ways. One subset spoke of their involvement with the *Worldwide Candle Lighting.* Another group mentioned their involvement with the local TCF newsletters. Others gave these accounts:

- One person mentioned her past role as the 'card angel' for her local TCF chapter when she *sent cards to families on their children's birthdays and on the anniversaries of their death.*
- The Chapter Leader for the TCF Sarasota Chapter helps coordinate *events to honor all of our Angels, especially the Dove Release in October.*
- One bereaved mom in Michigan *is part of a craft group through TCF that shows others how we can keep our child's memory alive by making special items with our hands.* She stays *involved with TCF because there were people who were there for me.*

In connection with the December candlelight services, Adam's mother noted that her leadership involvement with the event *gives me a way to get through that month and makes me feel good to do something for other families who have lost children. Also, I feel as if I am spending time doing something for my son like I did when he was still here with us.*

In addition to The Compassionate Friends, numerous other important organizations were mentioned by the *Survey Responders,* including: Bereaved Parents of the USA, Remembering Our Children, and Angel of Hope.

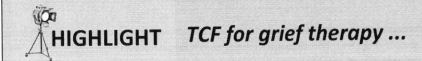

HIGHLIGHT *TCF for grief therapy ...*

One *Survey Responder* lost his 21-year old daughter in a car accident in 1978. Three weeks after that tragic event, his 23-year old daughter and 3-year old grandson died in a house fire. In terms of regular tributes, he writes about each of them on their birth dates and death dates in The Compassionate Friends (TCF) newsletter. He went on to share some information about his service to TCF:

I do not have a website. I belong to The Compassionate Friends and have been editor for our monthly newsletter for 30 years ... Our chapter was organized in October 1983, and my wife and I attended the first meeting. I was elected as treasurer, and 30 years later I still hold that position. I have been Chapter Leader for 20 of the 30 years our Chapter has been in existence ...

My wife had so many nervous breakdowns after the children's deaths that she was hospitalized for two and a half years all together. After six months in TCF, her doctor released her, saying that they did more for her in six months than he did in five years. I vowed then that I would never leave this group as long as I can help just one person through their grief like we were helped.

Let me close this section on helping others with three other examples of charitable activity. The first example is <u>not</u> about helping others who have lost a child – it is about helping others who are on a similar journey, in this case involving infants in a Pediatric ICU:

● *We take Kleenex boxes up to our PICU where Seth was for 85 out of his 100 days. I print a label that says we're fellow sojourners on the PICU journey and praying for them. Have a 'soft cry' on us … (because the hospital kleenex is so awful!)*

The second example is meant to address a dimension that is often unspoken, and that is something found across the social services – that is, when people helps others, they help themselves. This sentiment is expressed by Erika's mom:

● *I was chapter leader for my Compassionate Friends chapter for over five years where I helped other parents wind through this journey … I think they helped me more than I them.*

Then, thirdly, there was one individual – Ashley's father – who *wrote, recorded, and released 4 CDs of songs about Ashley, the grief journey, and finding hope again.* He also *performed and presented music and workshops in 900 U.S. cities for grief and loss organizations.* Ashley's father's name is Alan Pedersen, and he has brought great leadership to TCF as its current Executive Director. (See **SPOTLIGHT on Alan Pedersen** on the following pages for more information.)

SPOTLIGHT

Encounters with Alan Pedersen ...

The first time I met Alan Pedersen, it was online – I was doing some sort of grief-related google search and came across someone who mentioned a song that really lifted her spirits. It was called *One More Yesterday,* and it was attributed to this guy Alan Pedersen. I tracked down a free mp3 version, listened to it, and by evening I had a few songs by Alan that I played for my wife, adding *Angels Are Forever* and *Daddy Smile.* Alan passed our 'cry test' with flying colors – both of us cried profusely, with good tears.

The second time I met Alan was in his response to the *Tributes Survey.* I didn't know Alan from Adam (other than as a purveyor of heart-warming songs), but his name was on the email list that I used for the survey. He not only responded to the survey, but he also replied directly to my email. I knew he had to be 'somebody' when he wrote, 'While I can't post or promote any survey that isn't generated from within our organization, there are some things I can do personally to help solicit others to participate ...' Anyway, I checked into it, and Alan at that time was serving as Interim Director of The Compassionate Friends (TCF) – the organization often mentioned in this report that supports bereaved families in a variety of ways.

The third time I met Alan, I actually met him, although he won't remember me. It was in a receiving line at TCF's 2014 annual conference, held in Chicago that year, not far from my home. We sponsored the Book Store at the conference in my daughter Emma's name, and that got us an invitation to a reception where Alan, now the official Executive Director for TCF, was busy chatting and shaking hands.

I mention these different occasions because I know that I am not the only one who has felt better off as a result of meeting Alan at various points along the bereavement path. I am one among thousands and, on each occasion, Alan touches you in a comforting way. He meets you where you are and makes a helpful difference.

In terms of his own path, Alan has worn many hats – stand-up comedian, network radio news reporter, award-winning songwriter, and recording artist. A defining role for Alan is the one that began in 2001 when his 18-year-old daughter, Ashley, died in a car accident. As a bereaved father, Alan was virtually overwhelmed by grief until he began to find comfort, healing, and hope at his local chapter of TCF.

In 2003, to do something meaningful to honor and remember his daughter, Alan set out on a road trip to share his story, music, and hope with the grieving families he met at other TCF chapters across the country. That trip was but a first step in what's become a much bigger journey for Alan – one that's just as much about helping other bereaved families as it is about remembering Ashley. Alan has said, 'We were put on this earth to love them for as long as <u>we</u> live, not for as long as <u>they</u> lived.'

In addition to the current TCF Executive Director, Alan is a certified Grief Services Provider who has shared his story – through his songs, as a keynote speaker, or as a workshop presenter – at nearly 1,000 events. His music has been played at countless memorials, including events at Ground Zero, Columbine High School, and Virginia Tech University. Alan lives in Roseville, California, with his wife Denise, who is also a Certified Grief Specialist and bereaved mother to Sean, her 21-year-old son who died in 2004.

Families establish organizations to extend their reach.

A number of responders mentioned creating a nonprofit or some other kind of organization to extend their reach and impact in the chosen areas of focus.

For example, Joseph's family *started a nonprofit charity called Bikers Against Drugs* – *his dad is hoping my charity can prevent just one death from drug and alcohol abuse ...* Leslie's sister *created a group that does 5K and 10K walks/runs ... living Leslie's legacy one step at a time ...* And Christopher's mom is in the process of *starting a local chapter to help prevent suicide ...*

David's family created *a foundation through our community foundation and just this year we were able to start giving monies out of that fund. Another way to take David's legacy forward and honor his name, his life and his memory.*

And here are a couple of examples that carry the name of the child being honored:

♦ The **Tony Brown Foundation** is *dedicated to helping the bereaved heal and move forward.*

♦ The **Buckle Up for Perry and Justin** organization helps *spread awareness on the importance of buckling up.*

Lastly, there is a young woman whose name is Toni. Toni was brutally murdered at the age of 22 by her boyfriend in an incident of domestic violence. Toni's mother shared:

🩸 *We have created a nonprofit called **The TONI Connection** where we share information on dating violence and interpersonal relationships for teens and young adults. We want to honor who Toni was and share how she died to help prevent another family from going through the same trauma that we experienced following her death.*

Families award scholarships in honor of their children.

Many families have honored their children by granting scholarships to others and have felt satisfaction from doing so. As Sarah's mother noted, *Investing in a child's future feels good* ... Jo's mom expressed a more pragmatic perspective when she wrote that, separate from the good purposes that scholarships serve, the annual scholarship is *a way to count the years* ... and *seventeen scholarships have been presented so far.*

Within this reporting group, most of the scholarships were created by families that lost kids who were in high school or college at the time of death. Consistent with an overall theme of this report, the scholarships created by responders to the *Tributes Survey* have been designated in a variety of ways.

Most of the scholarships mentioned are intended for graduating high school students, although some are aimed at the college level. Also, most of them are targeted to certain attributes or merits (as opposed to financial need) of the recipients. Some of the scholarships are based on academics, others are based on different qualities. Here are some of the scholarships reported, in various categories:

Personal Qualities

- *We created an annual memorial scholarship for a talented high school senior who shares **characteristics** with our daughter.*

Specific Skill & Interest Areas

- *Each year we give two scholarships to students who will study **music** – one at a junior college and one at a four-year college.*
- *We award a **music** scholarship to a graduating high school senior who made a contribution to the school's music program. It is special because music was one thing that was right for my son when everything else was wrong.*
- *We have established a scholarship with the local **4H program** in his name.*
- *We established a **nursing** scholarship in Darcy's name.*

Athletics

- *We established a **wrestling** scholarship at Mike's high school.*
- *We fund a scholarship given to an athletic student at the high school who played a **sport** Brandon played and is in need of assistance for college.*
- *Beth Ann was a **softball** player, and it was her senior year in high school. So, we give a $500 scholarship to a senior softball player.*
- *A Brooke E. Joslyn Memorial Scholarship Fund was set up in his memory at Lafayette Central Catholic High School, which honors two high school **student-athletes** every spring. Brooke was an assistant*

basketball coach at the high school and loved helping the boys be the best they could be in their sport. To be considered for the scholarship, students need to display a good work ethic, good grades, and school and community involvement as a student-athlete.

HIGHLIGHT

A pig roast for scholarship ...

Each year, we host a pig roast at our home to raise money for a scholarship that is given to one or more seniors who are going to school for a career that focuses on working closely with people each day. It has been a wonderful blessing to us to be able to do this. Our first scholarship was given to one of Brittany's classmates. She would have graduated in 2008.

Friends & Family

- We set up some scholarships at my **church**.
- We set up two at his **school** – one in Justin's name and one in the driver's name
- We donated annually to college education funds for our ten **nieces & nephews** in memory of our daughter. Our daughter died before college age.

One family did mention that financial need was the basis for their scholarship. They reported, *We set up a scholarship fund for those in* **need** *in my son's name. Friends and family donate annually and it's comforting to know Michael is helping others make a life for themselves.*

Family members realign personal values and behaviors.

I have likened the loss of a child to a major amputation – a situation involving significant loss where you are permanently affected, fundamentally altered. After the initial trauma and after the scar tissue has formed, you still can never be the same. But it doesn't mean you can't live forward – you just live differently, you accommodate the change, and you compensate for the loss.

In a very real sense all of us who are so similarly afflicted have to find a 'new normal', and some of us find that our new normal includes paying tribute to our lost children in identifiable ways.

Sometimes the new normal includes things that make people feel good inside. One mom modifies her morning routine on some days along these lines. As she says, *I like to pay it forward. At Starbucks or Jamba Juice, I buy a gift card then give it to the cashier with a small piece of paper that says 'in loving memory of Carissa Lynn Thompson.' And then I order what she would have when she went there and ask them to give it to the next person who comes through.*

In a similar 'pay it forward' activity, another mom randomly pays for meals of people she doesn't know. And Beth Ann's mother gives parents in her area who lose children a special 'rub stone' for them *to keep in their pocket throughout the day leading up to the funeral and visitation.*

Beyond performing various acts of kindness, others are inspired to be better as a result of their loss. The first tribute that one mother mentioned on the survey was simply, *I improved my health.* And, in the opinion of Michelle's mom, *I think that the biggest tribute I can pay my daughter Michelle is to carry her memories forward and try to love everyone I meet in the spirit of the way Michelle treated them.*

There is one final aspect to this that I would like to touch on. To do so, let me refer to a statement I made in the first paragraph of this section: *It doesn't mean you can't live forward – you just live differently, you accommodate the change, and you compensate for the loss.* That sounds good, and it's easy to write, but it is way easier said than done. Some in the bereaved community find it very difficult, if not impossible, to accommodate the change and consequently may not 'live forward' the way some others do. And keep in mind that there is no right or wrong in any of this.

But there were a few *Survey Responders* who directly addressed this notion of living forward – implying, in a sense, that growing out of grief into a new normal (albeit compromised and diminished) can be a tribute in and of itself.

Jacob's mom stated it this way – *I have decided to live my life again – instead of just sitting around longing to be with him in heaven.*

Leslie's mom stressed the ongoing responsibility to others – *I think it is important to keep living and not forget about the other siblings left behind.*

And, lastly, one parent, whose son Michael passed away 29 years ago, takes a long view – *There comes a point where you feel like you just can't place the picture and light a memory candle anymore, because it prolongs the grief process ... I don't like to be reminded of those days ... I keep his memory in my heart.*

Chapter 6

Healing Effects of Tribute Activity

Then along came the Special Olympics – a beautiful blessing for these children and their parents. Indeed, we appreciate the confidence God placed in us, to send Robin our way.

— Dale Evans Rogers, Robin's Mom

6. Healing Effects of Tribute Activity

In view of all of this tribute activity, it seems natural to wonder about the impact of these tributes on the families and friends who organize and participate in them. So, on the inspiration of my (psychologist) daughter Sarah, I asked in the survey, *As you reflect on the time that has passed since the loss of the child, how would you say that tributes to the child have helped in the healing process?*

Most of the group (75%) responded to this question, and most of the *Survey Responders* had favorable things to say.

Bereaved families feel that tributes help the healing process.

There were a handful of people who candidly shared that they have not experienced a sense of healing from tribute-related activities. One person said, for example, that the tributes are *nice* but help *very little.* For another person, it was *hard to say. I do not feel healed.* Another commented, *I don't think the tributes have helped to ease my loss. It is still such a struggle.* And Sheldon's mom offered this view on the assistance from tributes: *Helped? Nah ... it still hurts like yesterday. I just cope in a new normal, just not the one I wanted.*

Kristi's mom associated tributes with healthy grieving but noted that the aftermath of her daughter's death delayed the grieving process. She reported, *I was thrown into court immediately after her death. For the next six years, I did not grieve ... My tributes were minimal, and I regret that.*

For the most part, though, people have found healing comfort of some sort in activities to honor their lost children. Perry's mother gave this perspective on benefits from tributes:

I don't believe you ever heal after you lose a child, because a part of you is missing and there is a big hole that can never be filled again. But I do believe you can learn how to function in this new life we have, and learn new ways to incorporate our children that have gone before us into our lives now.

In describing the positive impact of their tributes, a number of people used such short-word responses as ... *absolutely ... greatly ... very much ... DEFINITELY! ... immensely... tremendously! ... extremely helpful ...*

Others were also succinct in their responses by offering short, summary perspectives:

- *It gives me an opportunity to remember.*
- *I really think any tribute allows us to feel love – and love helps healing.*
- *Everything helps ... We need a lot of help.*

Some people responded in a general way about the influence of the tributes:

- *They have brought comfort and peace. We have learned to focus on the good memories that we have, and her love is still touching us and all of her family and friends.*

- *They have brought incredible healing. Especially considering the time that has passed. To see others come together and speak his name, remember his character, and love and laugh together has been ointment to a broken heart.*

The family context is important for sustaining the child, and a few respondents addressed the importance of tributes to dynamics in the surviving family. One respondent wrote: *We have benefited from working together in our family on memorial projects.* Another echoed: *They help tremendously, especially with helping our other children cope with the loss.*

Not surprisingly, most of the healing benefits cited by members of bereaved families in the *Tributes Survey* parallel the three categories that we have used to organize the tributes themselves: 1) to keep the children present, 2) to remember the children, and 3) to create goodness from loss.

Tributes to keep the children present have helped ... by just doing it!

For some people, the very act of taking action – just **doing something** – has been helpful.

- *The tributes help by making us proactive. It gives us something 'to do' rather than just sitting and letting the feelings of deep grief overwhelm us. So much of this is out of our control and, by 'doing' something, it gives us a sense that we can contribute in a meaningful way.*

One stressed a strengthened sense of connectedness.

- *The tributes help to link the world of the spirit with my reality. I feel connected to my son though he is no longer with me.*

One put it in terms of maintaining sanity.

- *Without all of the planning I've been doing for the water safety classes, I'd probably have ended up in a mental hospital. I've really devoted all of my extra time to these classes, and it's keeping me busy, focused, and off the floor.*

And another spoke favorably of the annual protocol involved in the memorial scholarship that the family awards.

- *It provides a very positive avenue for my energy ... I go to the awards night on the first Monday of May to meet the recipients of the scholarship. We take photos, and I share them with the donors the following year. This all helps me focus on positive things, people, and love of life that Brooke had.*

Tributes to keep the children present have helped ... by talking about the child

Several people mentioned the importance of talking about the child.

- *The tributes give way for conversations about the one that has been lost, which is healthy.*
- *The more that we talk about our child, the more it helps us to heal.*
- *People still tell me stories of my son and just talk to me about him. These are the best tributes! Talking about him has made me feel like he isn't really that far away. So, yes, it has helped me immensely.*

Tributes to keep the children present have helped ... by allowing the children to live on in our hearts

Sustaining the influence that a lost child has on our current lives is so important. Adam's mother stated it this way: *I feel that keeping his memory alive helps to keep him with us.* Others had similar feelings and expressed them in these ways:

- *The tributes keep me feeling like she is still a part of this world.*

- *Knowing our daughter still has a place in the world is comforting.*
- *These tributes are crucial to us. We feel that in this way Alex's love continues in this world, and Alex's life continues to make a difference and have importance and meaning.*
- *Most importantly, I see that she is still an inspiration to others!*
- *Marcella continues to give even though she is not here.*
- *Tiffany will always be a part of our family.*
- *The tributes help by allowing me to share his life with others.*
- *The tributes help us feel like we are passing on his light ... even if it isn't truly here.*

Tributes to remember the children have helped ... by keeping the memories alive

The most frequent comments from the group about the beneficial impact of tributes cluster around the concept of **remembering**.

- *It keeps her memory alive.*
- *Knowing that others remember helps.*
- *I want her to always be remembered ... I feel it helps to accomplish this.*
- *I have found great comfort in all these tributes knowing that we are keeping his memory alive.*
- *They help immensely as you realize that you are keeping his memory alive in order to introduce him to those who never met him.*
- *There's nothing more important than making sure he's remembered.*
- *It's always been about keeping her memory alive so that we feel as though her life was not in vain. It now continues and most likely will forever in her nieces and nephews.*

- *Remembering is healing.*

The flipside of remembering, of course, is **not forgetting**, and a number of family members expressed thoughts along this dimension.

- *It helps to know that others have not forgotten him.*
- *It always heals the hole that is in my heart a little bit each time I see or hear someone reflecting on Brittany. It helps to know that people do care and do not forget.*
- *When I'm having a bad day, I pay it forward, and it helps me to know she's not forgotten.*
- *My greatest fear is that Kelsey will be forgotten and that her life with us will not have meant anything. These tributes help to keep the spirit and memory with us.*

Tributes to remember the children have helped … by hearing the child's name

The simplest encapsulation of memories is in a **child's name**, and hearing it is a source of comfort to some.

- *Tributes help me in my healing because they keep Ashley's name and memory front and center.*
- *I love hearing people speak her name or ask questions about her, the colon cancer, or anything that lets me speak her name. Anything helps that keeps her memory alive and her name spoken.*

Tributes to create goodness from loss have helped … by renewing the sense of purpose, importance & meaning

In a complementary way, working on tributes provides some with a **sense of purpose**.

- *His fund gives us a reason to get up each morning.*
- *For me, doing something in honor and tribute for Kelsey provides me with a purpose and meaning in my life.*

A sense of purpose suggests critical importance, which a few people characterized using the concept of **'lifeline.'**

- *The tributes have been a lifeline, especially in the first few years. Early on, I sat by his memorial tree often and had conversations with him ... My Christmas Eve celebration with his friends continues to be a most important event in my life.*
- *Knowing after all these years that his friends still remember his birthday and death date ... and call me on holidays because I miss him so much ... has been a lifeline to my healing.*
- *I couldn't have made it without all of these activities.*

The parents who lost Dylan and Gavin also attest to the healing qualities of tributes with this perspective:

Tributes to our children mean the world to us. It is especially touching when others initiate it but, even when we personally organize such events (like birthday balloon releases), it helps us to know that others are still thinking of, missing, and remembering our boys. That will always remain very important to us.

The closing comment here goes to Toni's mom, who offered that the reason tributes are important to her is that they offer validation of Toni herself:

She lived, loved, and was important to others.

Chapter 7

Afterwords – a Forum for Sharing

I feel so helpless because I am.
(Aren't mommies supposed to kiss it and make it all better?)
You never get over it, but I've learned to cope.

— Carol Burnett, Carrie's Mom

7. Afterwords – A Forum for Sharing

What happens when you die? That's the unanswerable question, and 'afterlife' is the big enigma. So much in this is unknowable, but personally I believe that one important aspect of afterlife is what happens here in the land of the living <u>after</u> someone's <u>life</u> has ended. *How is that person remembered? What stories are told about that person? What endearing characteristics and qualities of the person are seen in other family members?* These questions all speak to the person's lasting impact on others and to the person's overall significance.

In this respect, families of children who have passed away have a special opportunity to continue their parenting and sustain their children in living memory by telling stories about them.

I call these stories **Afterwords**. In the publishing world, the *Afterword* follows the formal conclusion of the book, and it often takes the form of elaboration that sheds important light on the body of the work itself. That's what I have in mind when I think about the stories we tell about our lost children – that these are elaborations, after their lives formally concluded, that shed important light on our beautiful kids and help them be remembered.

One thing for sure about the *Tributes Survey* is that it demonstrates that bereaved families want to share *Afterwords* about their children – to tell their kids' stories – and we now know from the amazing sample of perspectives in this report that their stories are truly heartwarming.

Caring in Sharing

Much of this feeling derives from the notion: *There is caring in sharing.* As one couple of bereaved parents wrote, *We have learned that sharing our stories with other bereaved parents has been one of the most helpful parts of this terrible journey. We believe that we will continue to actively share and support other families who are presently living in similar situations, as well as those who will unfortunately someday find themselves living without one or more of their children.*

As I now look back on the *Tributes Survey* and this **Tributes Report,** I can clearly see that is exactly what this survey and the report of survey results turned out to be about – promoting the sharing of stories within the bereaved community about our lost children. I did not have this in mind when I first started out, but it makes perfect sense now that the collective story in this report is complete.

This might be what Brian's mom meant when she shared, *Telling our stories helps to keep our children alive in our hearts, and ONLY we know what that means ... Parents need to find each other and gather strength.*

Other *Survey Responders* expressed similar notions:

- *Keep their memory alive. They may be gone, but they're not forgotten.*
- *I can't emphasize enough the importance of saying their name and sharing something in their spirit with others, for a long time if possible.*
- *I firmly believe that sharing the memories and love of your child is a gift not only to others but to your own heart as well.*

Parting Words

In the *Tributes Survey,* the catch-all question at the end to capture things that became top-of-mind to the responders as they completed the survey was phrased as follows:

Lastly, space is provided here for anything else that you would like to share about paying tribute to our lost children that was not covered by the other questions on this survey.

Most of the responses collected by this question have been integrated into other sections of the **Tributes Report**. But, as this specific forum for sharing reaches closure, here are few thoughts to complete the *Afterwords* on our children who have passed away.

The hurt continues ...

- *My heart hurts anytime I think of the losses, so I have to keep working.*
- *Losing a child is the ultimate and, naturally, only ones who have lost a child understand that there is never closure to losing a child, especially as you get older and remember the previous birthdays, holidays, vacations and just life adventures with your child. Nothing is the same without them here in our lives. The grief lightens up, but the hurt never goes away. They are missed with everything we do in life from now on.*

Stay connected ...

- *Keep talking about them. Keep talking to them.*
- *Speak to them in your prayers or thoughts as you did before they passed over. They will hear you and will answer in their own way, and you will know when that happens. Just be open to the experience and do not question it. Just be thankful when it does.*

On tributes to the children ...

- *Before jumping to a memorial right away, think about what your child would like or what they liked to do. It's their memorial, not yours. Keep it simple, and involve friends and family in planning.*
- *Do whatever you feel would work for you.*
- *Each child is different, each death unique ... The most important tribute is that others continue to speak the name of our child, to continue to tell stories and jokes about the times when they were here ... that they never forget them, because we won't.*
- *It's not about how elaborate your tribute is. It is about honoring your child in a positive way!*
- *For many folks, it might be as simple as making their favorite birthday cake and meal on their birthday, creating a memorial garden or even a corner of their garden, planting plants whose cultivar names include their child's, to creating foundations ... But, in all the families I have spoken with, their eyes light up when they share. It seems to me that this sharing is a very important, helpful way to integrate their grief into their lives.*

Conclusion

As you now know, there is too much in this report to try to sum it all up in one pithy take-away observation. But, if pressed on what I think ties this all together, it's this:

Bereaved families want to honor their lost children with demonstrations of undying love.

Our children have died, but the love that we feel for our children will never die, and we will express this love in ways that feel right to us in honoring their lives and sustaining their memories.

In the end, I defer to a comment from the mom and dad in the survey who reported on two lost children. In answer to the question about special remembering places in the home, Dylan & Gavin's parents shared,

We continue to have our sons' belongings in many of the same places where they always would have been while they were both here with us … There's the constant mix of emotions between feeling how our children blessed us in this lifetime and the sadness and longing of missing them and longing for them to continue to be living in this world along with us … It is special to us to have items and pictures because we continue to love our sons dearly, and always will.

Backstories
A. Author Notes
B. Tributes Survey

I would give anything.
There's no price I wouldn't pay
for one more yesterday.

— Alan Pedersen, Ashley's Dad

Backstory A – Author Notes

In providing a personal wrap-up to **Tributes to Lost Children**, I would like to elaborate briefly on a few aspects of the perspective that I brought to bear as I worked on this project.

Value of 'Professional Dispassion'

In much of my life's work, I have found value from applying something I learned from my father (Tom), who was a physician. In the medical world, professionals pretty much have to do their work with something that my dad called 'professional dispassion.' What he meant by the phrase is that, in order to be effective, you have to be able to park your emotions – at least until the analytical/technical work is done. When you proceed with 'professional dispassion,' it doesn't mean that you don't care. Once the work is done, there may then be time for emotions, moods, questions and differences of opinion, and other expressions of passion. But the essential work is done without the clouding impact of personal feelings, biases, and preferences.

In this project, I was grateful for the proficiency with professional dispassion that I developed over the years, because I needed to park a lot of emotion as I worked with the tribute comments that people shared. I was not always successful – I think that's one of the reasons that it took me so long to complete this report. As I am on my own grief journey, I found myself taking various emotional detours as I processed through the tribute experiences of others. (Detours have become part of the 'new normal.') In the end, however, I feel as though I accomplished my mission, which was to present a complete, unbiased summary of what the survey families provided to me.

I started the project with questions that stemmed from my own curiosity. I do not have an agenda to promote, a theory to espouse, or any vested interest in one way of doing things over another. Even to the extent that this book is concerned, any net revenues that it may generate will be plowed back through the Foundation into the promotion of tributes and stories related to our wonderful departed children.

Hopefully, as a report-back to the survey participants, **Tributes to Lost Children** will be regarded as a fair and balanced presentation that provides insight into some of our motivations as a bereaved community and sheds light on the many ways we express the continuing love we feel for our departed children. I encourage readers to let me know how they agree or disagree with this assessment – just send me an email via *starmaster@starshinegalaxy.org.*

A 'Snapshot' in Time

In this context, I would like to elaborate on one of the words in the subtitle of this report. The subtitle is *A snapshot of how 147 families have honored their children who have passed away,* and the word that I would like to focus on is 'snapshot.'

The word 'snapshot' suggests that it is something that captures one moment in time, and that is exactly how this book is positioned – as a profile of what some 147 specific families have done as of a specific moment in time. The reason for the extra attention here is that I do not want readers to think more of this book that it is meant to be. I have been careful not to overgeneralize observations that are made in this report. Also, I do not pretend that the framework that I have developed is valid for all families at all times. (In fact, I hope that more people will share information so that we can continue to develop and refine the framework over time.) Perhaps most important, I do not mean to suggest in any of this that families <u>should</u> do one thing or another for whatever reason. You will rarely, if ever, see the 'should' word from me when it comes to grieving.

As far as generalizations are concerned, I have attempted to generalize only when there is a majority sense of the *Survey Respondents* as a group. For example, in the chapter on ***Healing***, I observe that: 'Bereaved families feel that tributes help the healing process.' Readers should recognize comments such as this as generalizations and understand that there are almost always exceptions. In this example, there were responders who reported that they do not feel healing from tribute activity. (This is typified by the comment, *I don't think the tributes have helped to ease my loss. It is still such a struggle.*) When the exceptions are significant, I have tried consistently to make note of them in the report.

My only vested interest, that underlies all of this tribute activity, is to honor the memories of children who have passed away and to celebrate their lives. With this in mind, I have tried to pass on virtually <u>everything</u> that <u>every</u> family responder had to share – in the <u>original</u> words they used to share. This is what gave rise to the ***Tributes Framework*** – as a way of organizing <u>all</u> the things that the families contributed. Consistent with this full inclusion goal, I took virtually no license with the words that *Survey Responders* used in answering the survey questions, other than to correct obvious spelling and punctuation errors. (I also occasionally have added a word or two to bridge thoughts, and I have sometimes used excerpts of responses, but hopefully never out of context.)

An Obvious Bias?

Because of this orientation on my part, I hope readers will find that my treatment of the information has been neutral and complete, balanced and fair ... with one possible exception. While I have tried not to impose myself (and my emotions) in this story much at all, I may have made a few too many references to my daughter Emma for some readers' liking.

If you find and object to my failings along these lines, please chalk them up to a father's pride in a beautiful and vibrant young lady known for teaching others how to shine.

Sealed with a kiss
from DOD (dear old dad)

✳ ——— *Special Events* ——— ✳

JUST DAD'N ME
Make some memories . . . Dads and daughters come dressed in your Sunday best and have a special evening including refreshments, dancing, entertainment and photos. **Please note: Dinner will not be served.**

$17 (n/r $26) per couple   1 day
$10 each additional child
Age/Grades: 4 yrs. - 6th grade
SE 7800-01   Su   2/13   5:30-7:30 pm   GHS Gym

Backstory B – Tributes Survey

> **Important Note:** The *Tributes Survey* is open (indefinitely) for new information on tributes to lost children. We will report new tribute information on the Starshine Galaxy Foundation website (see *starshinegalaxy.org),* in periodic updates to this report, and in other appropriate ways.
>
> **Complete the *Tributes Survey* at:** *https://www.surveymonkey.com/r/tributes-to-lost-children*

The *Tributes Survey* came about as a result of my curiosity regarding what other families have done to honor their kids who have passed away. It was one of those backburner items that I finally acted on in the January/February 2014 timeframe. Just a month or so before that, I wrote a poem that I shared with a fairly large number of individuals (500 or so) who were identified as coordinators for the 2013 Worldwide Candle Lighting activity organized by The Compassionate Friends (TCF). The poem was called, *Santa lost a child,* and I thought it was something that people might want to read as part of their candle lighting activities. (For anyone interested, the poem may be found on the *starshinegalaxy.org* website.)

Anyway, when I started acting on the survey idea, I used that same email list, figuring that virtually all of these folks either lost a child and/or knew people who did and so would be good candidates for sharing information about things that have been done in the past to pay tribute to children who have died. Using the online Survey Monkey tool, I put a survey together, sent out a survey link to the email list that I had compiled, and invited people to share their experiences and perspectives.

Of course, I had no idea how many of the ~500 people would respond, but I let it go for a week and, when I checked on the survey response, I saw that 147 families had responded without any prompting on my part. That puts the official response rate at 31%, which is pretty good right out of the chute, and I thought it would give me plenty of data to work with on a preliminary basis to get a feel for how people were responding.

Survey Population	
Survey email	04/26/14
Targeted recipients	471
# of records	147
Response rate	31%

As it turned out, the *Survey Responders* had <u>much</u> to say, and my plate quickly overflowed with data from this initial group. In the final analysis, that first group of 147 family representatives provided all of the data used to compile this report.

Design of the Tributes Survey

The *Tributes Survey* itself remains open and available for people to complete if they have tributes to lost children to report. The survey is also available for people to review from a research design perspective. The following link should take you to the active survey webpage:

https://www.surveymonkey.com/r/tributes-to-lost-children

In general, the design of the *Tributes Survey* is simple and straightforward. First of all, I gathered some information about the children and their family representatives, but I intentionally kept this to a minimum. (The loss of a child is very much a personal and private matter and, out of respect for the privacy of families who shared information, I considered it important to maintain focus on the tributes.)

Beyond that, I designed the survey to solicit information in four major slices, with the questions noted here:

1. Special Places of Honor

◆ *Did you create a special place for photos and other remembrances of the child?*
  – *If you have a name for this special place, what do you call it?*
  – *Can you describe this place and what makes it special?*

2. Online Memorials

◆ *Have you created an online memorial for the child?*
  – *How would you describe the online memorial that you created?*
  – *Did you use an established website? What website did you use? Would you recommend this memorial website to others? Why or why not?*

3. Tributes

◆ *Describe the things that you have done to honor or pay tribute to the child, and indicate what made each activity so special.* [SPACE IS PROVIDED IN THE SURVEY FOR THREE DIFFERENT TRIBUTE ENTRIES]
◆ *If you are planning a new tribute to the child but haven't completed it yet, please describe what you are planning.*
◆ *If someone other than you or your family paid a tribute to the child that you thought was especially meaningful, please describe that tribute here.*

4. Healing

🔸 *As you reflect on the time that has passed since the loss of the child, how would you say that tributes to the child have helped in the healing process?*

Data Analysis Plan

As you can see in these four major topic areas, the most substantive questions were phrased to solicit open-ended responses. Given the prolific nature of the responses received and the content-rich character of many entries, the most challenging aspect of data analysis was managing these free-text elements. Since they are not easily quantifiable, my work relied on the communication research technique referred to as 'content analysis.'

In this case, the 'tribute' is the base unit of analysis, and the research effort involves disassembling the text responses to the lowest level that represents a discrete tribute, then tagging it with one or more category and subcategory codes. For example, the response – *Created a memorial garden at our home, with pond full of koi, a waterfall, and butterfly attracting plants around the pond. Butterflies are a symbol and a sign to us.* – was treated as one tribute. This one tribute, however, was given two codes – 1-3 and 1-4, as follows:

<u>Category</u>	<u>Subcategory</u>
1. Tributes to Keep Present	3. Outdoors
1. Tributes to Keep Present	4. Signs & Symbols

Once the coding of the text-based material was complete, the individual data elements were organized into a format that was then amenable to assessment and observation, grouping and sequencing, and eventual reassembly into a report format that would provide an overall 'story' that could be meaningful to others.

I wish I could say that I divined the **Tributes Framework** – the overall 'story' structure – right from the beginning and consequently then say that all of the pieces just fell into place. Unfortunately, that is far from the truth. There were numerous iterations all along the course of writing the report before I felt that I got it right. That 'right story' – in the form of the organizing framework of this report – is shown in a skeletal format on the opposite page. This presents the 'big picture' in a concise way. (Note that a decorative one-page version of this outline is FREELY available for download on the Starshine Galaxy Foundation NFP's website. Please visit *starshinegalaxy.org* to find this resource.)

A final word: To echo a point that I made in **Chapter 2 – Meet the Children**, I make no pretense that what I have compiled is the 'be all, end all' on what drives bereaved families or what they do to honor their children who have passed away. It just seems to make sense for the information that I gathered from the *Tributes Survey.* As I processed through the survey responses, I was after one thing – a good answer to the question:

What is the storyline that unites all of the Survey *responses in a way that most honors the information that 147 families so graciously shared about their children – the heroes and heroines of **Tributes to Lost Children**?*

This report is my answer to that question.

The 'Tributes Framework'

from **Tributes to Lost Children** – by Rod Mebane, Emma's Dad

– a snapshot of how 147 families have honored their children who have passed away –

1	**TRIBUTES TO KEEP PRESENT**		Bereaved families want to keep the children present in their lives ...

1	**ALTARS**	they build 'altars of remembrance' to keep their children close
2	**IN HOUSE**	they dedicate areas in the home to create special places of honor
3	**OUTDOORS**	they create outdoor areas around the home for peaceful reflection
4	**SIGNS & SYMBOLS**	they associate presence of their children with iconic signs
5	**INVOLVEMENT**	they continue to involve their children in ongoing activities

2	**TRIBUTES TO REMEMBER**		Bereaved families want their children to be remembered ...

1	**PLACES**	they designate special places for community remembering
2	**NAMESAKES**	they promote the children's names
3	**CREATIONS**	they create expressive works inspired by the children
4	**MEMORIALS**	they participate in memorial activities
5	**DAYS**	they commemorate the children's special days

3	**TRIBUTES TO DO GOOD**		Bereaved families want some good to come from their losses ...

1	**DONATIONS**	they donate to meaningful causes
2	**CHARITIES**	they contribute to charitable activities related to the children
3	**OUTREACH**	they reach out to serve important purposes
4	**SUPPORT**	they provide grief support to others
5	**ORGANIZATIONS**	they establish organizations to extend their reach
6	**SCHOLARSHIPS**	they award scholarships in honor of the children
7	**VALUES**	they realign personal values and behaviors

starshinegalaxy.org

Share Your Thoughts

The *Tributes Survey* is open and available to anyone who would like to add to our research knowledge on tributes to children who have passed away. The following link should take you to the survey webpage:

https://www.surveymonkey.com/r/tributes-to-lost-children

We will be periodically updating our findings based on new information that people contribute, and we aspire to provide a permanent, free, online home for tributes and stories related to our departed kids. Please visit *starshinegalaxy.org* – the website home of the nonprofit Starshine Galaxy Foundation – for more information.

While at *starshinegalaxy.org,* share your tribute experiences, links to tribute articles and websites, questions, and ideas in general or send your thoughts via email to *starmaster@starshinegalaxy.org.* As you should know, we are <u>all about sharing</u>, and we will loop back with you as best we can.

Also, please feel free to share your tributes experiences, photos, comments, links, and more on our Facebook community page:

https://www.facebook.com/tributestolostchildren

IF YOU HAVE GOOD THINGS TO SAY about **Tributes to Lost Children**, PLEASE WRITE AN AMAZON REVIEW
Take two minutes to write a reader review on Amazon. Just navigate to Amazon, search for the title –
Tributes to Lost Children – and click on *'Write a customer review.'*

Thank you for spending time with these children. Their stories will continue to live on through you.

Made in the USA
Middletown, DE
19 February 2017